"We have a problem within the church that mos[t] [...] wives are not praying together. Men are not in[...] what to pray or how to pray. Sam and Vicki Ingrassia provide biblical g[...] book, *Praying Together*. Praying as a couple will change your marriage and will change your life."
—KERBY ANDERSON, host of the nationally syndicated talk radio show *Point of View*

"When I was profiling Sam and Vicki Ingrassia for a story on *The 700 Club*, what I found was a couple undergoing a two-person revolution. God was showing them, through praying His Word together, they could take their marriage to deeper spiritual and emotional intimacy. All it takes is you and your loved one looking down to the Word of God in your hands and looking up in prayer to the God of your marriage. You + your spouse + praying His Word = a spiritual intimacy and oneness every Christian couple can reach. You know what they say: testimony trumps theory. But in *Praying Together*, you're blessed to get both. Sam and Vicki show how prayer has brought deep friendship, fellowship, and fun to their own marriage, as well as many others . . . and how it can now do the same for yours."
—PAUL STRAND, CBN News senior Washington, DC, correspondent

"The need, in our culture and churches, has never been greater for authentic biblical marriages to prevail and demonstrate God's best plan for mankind. Biblically sound and genuinely successful marriages must be built upon and fueled by a vibrant life of prayer. *Praying Together* helps couples get beyond the inertia, guilt, and lack of skills that inhibit their prayer life together. This book provides the motivation and a model for success that will benefit any couple seeking a more meaningful life of spiritual intimacy. I can vouch for the veracity of their story and the efficacy of their teaching, having served closely in ministry with Sam and Vicki Ingrassia for more than 20 years."
—CURTIS V. HAIL, president and CEO of e3 Partners and I Am Second

"If you put into practice the principles from Sam and Vicki Ingrassia's new book, *Praying Together*, it will transform your marriage and establish your oneness stronger than it has ever been. Praying together as a couple is the single most important element of a marriage that is abundantly fulfilling and remains strong during the storms of life. *Praying Together* will help you set a solid foundation if you are newly married. If you have been married for years, it will help repair your foundation and make it new again. Pastor, this is the book you've been looking for in your premarriage counseling. Bible study leader, this is perfect for couples, no matter how long they have been married. Read this book, then grab your Bible, and hit your knees together as husband and wife."
—TOM DOYLE, author of *Killing Christians: Living the Faith Where It's Not Safe to Believe* and vice president of church and ministry partnerships and Middle East/North Africa director of e3 Partners

"I have been in ministry for more than 20 years, discipled hundreds, counseled countless marriages, and known the power of prayer on a personal level. Yet, even as a minister of the gospel,

I have failed to pray with my wife regularly. Unfortunately, it is the one thing that she desires more than almost anything else, to connect with me on the deepest level. For some reason, it is easier to lead a crowd in prayer than my spouse. Sam and Vicki are not calling us to a grand gesture, but to one loving step toward spiritual intimacy with our spouse. Filled with grace, compassion, and understanding, their book can help marriages take the ideal into reality. I highly recommend *Praying Together* for you as a couple, for your church, and for anyone who would listen."

—DAVID FUQUAY, lead minister of spiritual formation at Northwest Bible Church

"After 20 years of leading premarital counseling, I have arrived at the bottom-line advice I want all couples to follow: *put God at the center of your relationship*. When a couple consciously prioritizes their faith, it's a fountain of health that flows into every other area. I know what you're thinking: *duh*. But here's the reality: most couples have no clue how to actually do this. Even worse: 5, 10, 20 years into marriage, the cluelessness remains. Finally, with the Ingrassia's book, there is a tool I can put in the hands of every couple—engaged or married—that will actually equip them to do the main thing well."

—DAVE GUSTAVSEN, senior pastor of Jacksonville Chapel church

"In order for our marriages to be strengthened, husbands and wives must learn to pray together. If you need encouragement in this area of your life, Sam and Vicki Ingrassia's latest book, *Praying Together,* is a must read. This book shares why couples *should* pray together and teaches couples *how* to pray together. This call to pray together as husbands and wives has never been more crucial than it is now. If you want a stronger, healthier marriage, you'll gain incredible insight and wisdom from this book as to the power of praying together."

—JACK GRAHAM, pastor of Prestonwood Baptist Church

"Prayer is a rare commodity in the contemporary church and even more rare within the homes of many Christians. Sam and Vicki Ingrassia have a passion for prayer and specifically one where couples are praying together for their family, community, and world. I highly recommend this resource, which will rekindle your passion for prayer. Their work has had a tremendous impact on my marriage and my church."

—DR. KEN LANG, senior pastor of Calvary Chapel Syracuse church

"Marriage is a sacred relationship that is given to us by Almighty God. Christian couples know they should be experiencing spiritual intimacies with their spouse, but often don't know how to make it happen. There is no better way to invest in your marriage relationship than to pray Scripture together. Sam and Vicki Ingrassia experienced the ups and downs of spiritual intimacy in marriage for decades before God revealed a simple and doable plan for Sam to take the lead. The good news for you and me is that the challenge and model shared in *Praying Together* is biblical and timeless. Sam and Vicki teach you how to go deeper in your marriage by praying together with the Bible as your guide."

—MARC MCCARTNEY, missions pastor of Lake Pointe Church

"As a man who has failed and succeeded at leading my family, I want to encourage you to read (and apply) Sam and Vicki's teaching in *Praying Together* about reading Scripture and praying with your spouse. The Bible reminds us in Hebrews 4:12 that 'the word of God is living and active.' By applying the spiritual discipline of praying as a married couple with the Bible as your guide, you will see reconciliation, peace, love, intimacy, and the power of God unleashed in your individual lives, marriages, and families."

—MATTHEW MCINTYRE, CEO of Puritan Financial Companies

"In *Praying Together*, Sam and Vicki Ingrassia provide a balanced, realistic view from both husband and wife about the often-awkward attempt of couples to maintain a prayer life together. As with Sam's first book written to husbands, *Just Say The Word*, this expanded volume for couples provides a road map to strengthen relationships, repair marriages, and deepen intimacy between spouses—all through the simple act of regularly praying together. It's easy to say it, but it's hard to do it! Thankfully, Sam and Vicki have worked successfully to achieve this spiritual intimacy in their own lives and they are sharing this proven blueprint to help us get it done!"

—NORM MILLER, chairman of Interstate Batteries

"*Praying Together* is the fruit of many faithful years that Sam and Vicki Ingrassia have worked tirelessly for the sake of the gospel and for the strengthening of marriages and families within the body of Christ. We have known Sam and Vicki for almost two decades and have seen firsthand how their lasting and flourishing marriage has blessed not only our lives, but the lives of thousands of other couples as they have faithfully shared God's principles for marital unity through prayer. We heartily recommend *Praying Together* for any couple that longs for deeper spiritual intimacy with each other. It is practical, biblical counsel that will help you let go of past failures and move into an exciting future together."

—NATHAN AND PATTY SHEETS, co-owners of Nature Nate's Natural Honey

"Sam and Vicki have addressed the heart of the key issues confronting a husband and wife wanting to have a marriage that is all that God intends it to be. They have boldly, with great sensitivity, addressed the issue that most couples (and men who want to lead in their marriage) find difficult to do: that of praying together conversationally. Sam and Vicki have provided the key to experiencing the presence, power, and promises God offers to each couple that invites Him into their marriage on a regular basis. In all my years of marital counseling as a pastor, the one ingredient that kept couples together and strengthened marriages like no other is conversational prayer. In this book, Sam and Vicki offer practical and simple ways to help couples begin praying together using God's Word. This book should be recommended reading for all couples that want a marriage that experiences the power and blessings of God and continues to the next generation."

—DR. MARK (staff effectiveness director for Cru)
AND JANET STEWART

DEDICATION

To our daughters Christina, Nicole, and Stephanie

We are delighted to see God's handiwork,
fashioning each of you as special women of God.
The Lord has used each of you to teach us
unique and beautiful life lessons!

We love you dearly!

PRAYING TOGETHER

A Simple Path to Spiritual Intimacy for Couples

SAM AND VICKI INGRASSIA

NEW HOPE® PUBLISHERS
Gospel-Centered. Missions-Driven.

BIRMINGHAM, ALABAMA

New Hope® Publishers
PO Box 12065
Birmingham, AL 35202-2065
NewHopePublishers.com
New Hope Publishers is a division of WMU®.

Library of Congress Cataloging-in-Publication Data: 2016932819

ISBN-10: 1-59669-473-4
ISBN-13: 978-1-59669- 473-6

N164113 • 0516 • 2.5M1

CONTENTS

ACKNOWLEDGMENTS

To Jim and Kaye Johns of Prayer Power Ministries:
Thank you for your enduring encouragement and for walking with us in the extreme mountaintops and valleys of our lives—and everywhere in between! Your encouragement and guidance has been steadfast, reliable, and deeply personal. Your prayers have borne us along more than we likely realize. Your guidance and support helped bring *Just Say the Word* into reality, and your continuing encouragement fueled us to this next level with *Praying Together*.

To Curtis and Amy Hail of e3 Partners Ministry:
You thought God sent you to New Jersey to speak at Jacksonville Chapel about missions ministry—we could not have anticipated you were actually coming to deliver God's call upon our lives to focus on international Great Commission ministry. For sure we were a "ragtag band" in those initial formative years . . . but come to think of it, perhaps not much has changed—truly, it has all been about the sustaining grace of God.

To Nathan and Patty Sheets of Nature Nate's Natural Honey:
You were there in the earliest days when God broke into our lives with this message and model for marital prayer. The Lord has used you not only to help us launch this ministry, but over and over again you have been there to encourage us to keep going. All from a young

guy whom God would dare to bring to the "inner sanctum" of our powerful cabinet meetings!

To Jack and Elizabeth Reaves of Reaves Insurance Agency:

Your steady friendship and prayers have profoundly impacted each member of our family—if you doubt that, just ask any of our three daughters! If ever we need to call someone in the middle of the night, we would not hesitate to dial your number. God has given us multiplied special memories with you both on the foreign soils of spiritual harvest in Romania and Colombia, but also here at home. Since we met in that providential missions meeting years ago, you have walked with us in the realities of life. Thank you for consistently reminding us that the key of Christian life is "Christ in you the hope of glory!"

To Bill and Merle Jeanne Albert of Fellowship Greenville:

What can we say? It has been accurately said, "Some people come into your life for a time, some for a season, and some for a lifetime." When we arrived as a brand new, young pastoral family at Jacksonville Chapel—you were there. When we were called to Global Missions Fellowship—you were there. When we branded to e3 Partners and focused our work in Colombia—you chose to walk countless *barrios* to share the gospel of Jesus Christ and help establish simple churches. Thank you for your continual presence in our corner.

To Jason and Emily Morris of e3 Partners/Colombia:

Many times I have said, and I say it yet today, our ministry with e3 Colombia, with *Just Say The Word*, and now *Praying Together* would never have reached its potential without the creative energy and ideas you brought to the table—and the skills to pull it all together!

We are forever grateful for how you have faithfully served with us in yoke together.

To David Shepherd and Greg Webster
of New Vantage Partners:

From the first time we met you, we knew you were the men God sent to help us find our way down a path we could have never imagined. You not only patiently pointed us the right direction, but you led us, step by step to bring our conviction and testimony to the printed page. Because of your expertise and sage counsel, countless marriages have been challenged toward more intentional spiritual intimacy through Scripture praying. Thank you for laying the trail of crumbs before us so we could find our way in this adventure.

BUILDING ON A ROCK FOUNDATION

*I*s *this another marriage book?* you might be wondering. No, it's not really—but we are going to talk about intimacy in marriage.

Then this is a Christian life book? might be the next question that comes to mind, but it's not exactly that, either. Yet we are going to talk a lot about prayer.

Aha! Then this must be another book on prayer, right? Well, not just that.

OK, so what is it about?

It's about lifting a burden that may at times seem to smother your marriage relationship. And it's about a simple, doable path to shove off the weight, awaken fresh connectedness, and introduce new or *renewed* spiritual oneness in your marriage. We know both the before and after of what we're talking about.

NOT SEEING WHAT'S RIGHT THERE

A burden weighed on us. Although invisible to the eye, it was very real and very heavy. While we may have had a "good marriage"—some people would have even said a great marriage—this burden created seasons of tension, confusion, and heaviness. Much of the time, we didn't particularly notice it. Then at other times, we knew *something* was pressing on us, but we could never say quite what it was.

In God's providential timing, He pointed out what was wrong with the way we were running our race together, and almost immediately we suspected this burden was not unique to our marriage. Eventually, we became convinced that it does, in fact, weigh upon many—dare we say most—marriages in the body of Christ. It is even heavy upon Christian husbands and wives who help others find and pursue God—yes, even on people in ministry!

Sure, husbands and wives share "spiritual life" from time to time. We go to church, pray with our kids, and perhaps even manage occasional family devotions. We may teach Sunday School, lead a youth group, head up a Bible study, or even preach on Sunday mornings. We, the Ingrassias, were right there. However, at our home address something was missing, and we now know it's missing from many homes.

For many couples, the spiritual connection as husbands and wives is haphazard, intermittent, bumping along, and barely staying on the road. These days, husbands and wives often run fast on separate paths. We have differing, legitimate responsibilities to fulfill, depending on how they are arranged in any particular marriage, but the issue—the burden—is not caused by the different paths. The problem is the distance between our paths and the resulting spiritual disconnectedness. Different directions mean that our spiritual intersections are most likely infrequent. Distance creates the opportunity for nontogether things to muscle their way in. Yet Jesus warns that a "house divided against itself will not stand" (Matthew 12:25 NKJV), and the world, spiritual forces, and even our own flesh, are more than happy to see our houses divided unto destruction and demise.

LIFE GETS IN THE WAY

Demanding schedules, multiple jobs, a robust agenda of weekly activities, lessons of all sorts for our kids, carpools scurrying back and forth across town, and running to the airport for business trips all equal damaged connectedness. And stresses like more month left than money, another run to the emergency room, a job transfer, and fear, anger, depression, and insecurity rear up to unsteady our hearts. Life deals so many cards, we don't know how to fit them into our hands!

Jesus knew all about this and had a solution:

> *Therefore everyone who hears these words of mine and puts them into practice is like a wise man who built his house on the rock. The rain came down, the streams rose, and the winds blew and beat against that house; yet it did not fall, because it had its foundation on the rock. But everyone who hears these words of mine and does not put them into practice is like a foolish man who built his house on sand. The rain came down, the streams rose, and the winds blew and beat against that house, and it fell with a great crash.*
>
> —MATTHEW 7:24–27

The rain, rising streams, and blowing winds beat upon our marriages and families, but notice that Jesus does not offer any way to stop the storms from coming at us. No, He talks about how to build lives that will remain intact despite the onslaught. *Stability* is the reward for any house built upon a rock foundation, and it's up to us to make sure we build on rock, not sand.

So what has this got to do with the mysterious burden on marriage we mentioned earlier? Simply that God pointed out the invisible but very real burden we carried in our own marriage and showed us that we felt it because we were building on sand. The weight pressed down on us, and we were sinking in the soft stuff underfoot. But God also graciously revealed to us an answer. He showed how to unload the weight, experience new freedom, and gain fresh hope in our marriage and family.

With that, we started rebuilding our lives on the rock (no longer on the sand), and rather quickly, God's solution became a game-changer for us! There was healing, restoration, a reawakened spiritual life, a renewed passion for God, and new passion for *each other*. What fun!

What was the burden of ours, and why do we think you might be carrying it, too? It is the lack of intentional and regular spiritual connection as a married couple. There are multiple ways to foster spiritual health in our marriages. We specifically realized we were missing a fundamental ingredient of a spiritually sound marriage: *praying together as husband and wife*.

THE QUESTION

The key to unloading the burden is to ask an essential question. So, be honest when you answer. *Besides praying over meals, when you put your children or grandchildren to bed, or praying at a church-related gathering, how often do you pray together as husband and wife—just the two of you?*

Your answer is likely not a comfortable one. We know because of the answer from our own marriage over many years. Since we first asked ourselves that question, we have also posed it to innumerable Christian couples across multiple cultures and contexts, and we know how their answers come out. Never. Rarely. Occasionally.

Hardly ever. Not Enough. When needed. Clearly, there is a stark gap within marriages, even the ones we call "Christian."

Although prayer is ultimately a great mystery, there are many things we *do* know about it. Prayer is communication with the living God. And, prayer makes a difference. Since those two confessions are true, how can we bring prayer more vitally into our marriages? As husbands and wives, how can we cover our children with effective prayers? Praying off the tops of our heads usually leaves us praying the same things in the same way over and over again. We know we need to be more intentional and more regular in spiritual connection in our marriages. Yet, sometimes we feel mysteriously blocked from the very thing we need. The rains, rising streams, and blowing winds are relentless. We need a solid rock foundation.

This assertion is not meant to make you feel guilty in any way. We know you don't need more guilt. No, we intend for this book to give you hope! Still, it is important to recognize how we have stumbled, because the admission can give way to the repentance of mind and heart—the commitment to turn away from a failed past—that opens us to viable and lasting changes. Mourning the past (or even the present) will not provide long-lasting motivation and transformation.

We need to see something ahead: a vision for what could be. The opportunity is ripe for God-fearing husbands and wives to see the Lord show up in very real ways. Through what we've witnessed during the past few years, we believe God is surfacing this burden that troubles most Christian marriages—not so He can make us feel bad about ourselves but so He may have the opportunity to bring renewal to our lives and marriages.

Tucked in the heart of the Book of Joel among the minor prophets of the Old Testament, there is a hopeful truth of how the Lord can bring forth His grace to provide blessed restoration when we choose to turn toward him. Joel confronts the people of God in Judah through the reality of a locust plague that had devastated their crops. In an agrarian society, such loss had far-reaching consequences. The people of God found themselves under the sting of judgment, suffering great loss. Yet God calls his people to wake up and cry out to Him; to rend their hearts and return to the Lord. Then God declares, "I will repay you for the years the locusts have eaten" (Joel 2:25). In His grace God offers an exciting and hope-filled future!

In some seasons of life, we experience failure and feel time has been lost. Perhaps even years have been eaten away. A vast swarm of locusts have descended upon the fields of our lives, families, and marriages. But God is declaring that in His grace the lost harvest can be restored, if we will wake up, turn back, and cry out to Him.

This book shares our own personal story that resonates with both the painful loss and hope-filled restoration the prophet Joel describes. We also share a model and path for praying together in marriage, which is not only biblical but also simple to understand and implement. It will lead your marriage into a fresh dimension of spiritual intimacy. Praying together will bolster your marriage in the storms of life and increase your ability to equip and protect each other. It will also help you help your children and grandchildren live in Christ. It will touch every dimension of your lives.

JUST SAY THE WORD

God brought the question concerning how often we prayed together as husband and wife front and center in our own marriage. And we thank Him for doing so. Even though we had been engaged in Christian ministry for many years, we did not pray together very much as just husband and wife. In the pages that follow, we share our story, so that like us, you can step forward with hope and resolve to develop a fresh and vital spiritual connection in your marriage.

We first began to realize how widespread this need is when Sam wrote a short book for men, called *Just Say the Word: A Simple Way to Increase Your Passion for God and Your Wife,* in which he spoke to Christian husbands, man-to-man, about the lack of spiritual intimacy in most marriages. The response to Sam's book told us that Christian husbands everywhere were carrying the burden of knowing they were not cutting it spiritually in their marriages. But most men did not know what to do about it. For a variety of reasons, they simply felt stuck.

Although the purpose of *Just Say the Word* was to show husbands a manageable way to become more intentional and regular in connecting spiritually with their wives, we discovered that other factors also affect the vitality of spiritual intimacy in marriage and make a difference in how well "praying Scripture" can be implemented. God opened many doors for us to speak into couples' lives through churches, men's seminars, local and national radio broadcasts, television interviews, and online articles. Whether in the United States, in Colombia, or Romania—all places where we have personally ministered to married couples—a path was opening to us.

Because of our missions work with e3 Partners Ministry, *Just Say the Word* touched many marriages around the world, and the feedback has been profound and helpful. To give you a taste of what is happening, we've included comments from real men and women—and the results of their "praying together" experience—at the beginning of each chapter. The wealth of input we received and "upgraded" marriages we've seen have given us some remarkable new ideas that ramp up the effectiveness of praying the Word. That's why we've taken the next step to write this book.

From interacting with so many marriages over the last several years, dimensions of the *Just Say the Word* message have widened and deepened. And now, with that experience and our own growth well in progress, Vicki brings to light the wife's voice and perspective to shape a fuller dimension of the issue. The core premise, that the most effective prayer tool available is the Word of God itself, is still the baseline, but now we move on to a deeper level and to a wider audience of marriage needs.

God's purpose is holistic intimacy in marriage. Husbands and wives are meant to relate physically, emotionally, and spiritually without shame before one another and God. The path we propose in this book is meant to take you there. Praying together, using the Bible for guidance, will fuel vital and fulfilling intimacy.

Thank you for coming with us on the journey. Along the way, we ask you to ask God to speak to you and your spouse. You can use the sample prayers at the end of each chapter to get you started. And may God bless your growth as one.

START-UP PRAYER, GUIDED BY MATTHEW 7:24–27

Therefore everyone who hears these words of mine and puts them into practice is like a wise man who built his house on the rock. The rain came down, the streams rose, and the winds blew and beat against that house; yet it did not fall, because it had its foundation on the rock. But everyone who hears these words of mine and does not put them into practice is like a foolish man who built his house on sand. The rain came down, the streams rose, and the winds blew and beat against that house, and it fell with a great crash.

Father, the words of Jesus ring true in our experience. Right now in our lives, we are experiencing relentless rains, streams, and winds in different areas. We do not want to be like the foolish man; we do not want to build our house on sand. We know the outcome would be a collapse. We want to be wise men and women, wise husbands and wives! It is easy to see that Your rock foundation is what we need, but we often don't know how to secure that foundation. Lord, speak to us and show us a biblical and simple way to connect spiritually in our marriage—a way to build upon the Rock. In Jesus' name, amen.

CHAPTER 1

MIXED PAIRS
OR MARTIAL ARTS?

We recently invited Sam and Vicki Ingrassia to share their story about prayer in marriage at our conference. The feedback from that event was overwhelmingly positive. From the moment the event ended until today, people have made a point to share a story of how the idea of praying with their spouse is impacting their marriage. People were inspired to make changes and commitments in their marriages. What I personally loved was this model of praying Scripture as husband and wife is not calling us to a grand gesture but to one loving step towards spiritual intimacy with our spouse.

—PASTOR DAVID

TWO IMAGES, ONE RELATIONSHIP

If you have watched any Olympic ice-skating programs, you have likely heard commentary by Olympic men's gold medal skating champion Scott Hamilton. (Scott's story for Jesus Christ is on the website iamsecond.com.) We met Scott at an I Am Second ministry event in Dallas, where we heard firsthand the powerful testimony of his life and journey with Christ

We realized after talking with Scott that mixed-pairs figure skating offers a delightful and inspiring analogy to couples in a marriage.

The skaters glide over the glistening ice, harmonizing each move with just-right background music. Side-by-side, the union and flow of motion seems effortless. The man and woman each fulfill their roles in exquisite form. An anchor point, the man provides power and direction. He lifts his companion gracefully into the air while the couple spins together across their ice stage. The audience gasps as he tosses his partner forward into double and triple toe loops. The blades of her skates find the ice, and she lands as a mesmerizing smile belies the impossibility of the feat just completed.

Yet for all the man's strength and athletic prowess, all eyes are on the woman and her flawless beauty. Adorned with just enough sparkle and elegance to highlight her enchanting form, her natural connection to her partner and their craft make it hard to imagine her anywhere else. Were the transcendence of their moments on ice translated to all of life, any couple like them would surely experience heaven on earth! The image is extreme, to be sure, but an extreme to be adored.

Equally sure, though, is an opposite extreme. You may have seen marriages (or may be in one!) that look more like a martial arts match. The two people in the ring are *not* partners. Quite to the contrary—they are opponents! They do not intend to work together and, in fact, face each other to do battle. They spar or grapple in an intense and intentional power struggle, each seeking an advantage in order to overcome the other. Every strategic punch or kick has one goal: to dominate the opponent and win. There is no harmony to the movement of this couple.

A sad reality is that most of our marriages have occasions, or perhaps even seasons, when we feel more like opponents than partners. During these delicate times, ill-advised words, expressions, gestures, and emotions damage the relationship.

Even in "good" marriages, couples rarely glide unimpeded indefinitely. We may be in a season of harmony, but a test is just around the corner. And, fortunately, most marriages do not reflect only the martial arts extreme. Most of us are likely somewhere between these images. The question is: how can we move out of the ring and onto the ice? How can each of us see our spouse less as an opponent and more as a true partner?

As Christians, we know—at least in theory—that spiritual intimacy is the nuclear fuel of our relationship with God and with one another. But we need to find a reasonable and accessible path for more intentional and more regular spiritual connectedness. We need direction and some ways of finding that direction are more effective than others.

COMPASS OR MAP APP?

Suppose you wanted to go from Dallas to Atlanta but had only a compass to help you find the way. For starters, you would watch the compass needle wobble around under the glass pointing to true north, and then you would wander off in the direction of the "E." By heading east, you might eventually arrive in Atlanta—if you were lucky. Clearly, on a trip like this, a compass is not the best tool for guidance because it only indicates a general direction. But consider the difference offered by a smartphone map app.

Using satellites and precision mobile technology, a map app can pinpoint your exact location. Then, if you key in the address of your desired destination and touch the "route" button, the tech magic unfolds! Instantly, a green pin with a blue blinking dot shows where you are. A red marker pops in to pinpoint your destination. A blue path connects the pins to show exactly which roads lead to your destination. Most apps tell how long it should take to make the trip. You may even be able to choose from precisely drawn alternate paths. Finally, if you want, a voice with the accent of your choosing will tell you where to go turn by turn.

Often, though, the spiritual exhortations we receive are more like a compass than a map app. To achieve spiritual growth and maturity, we are encouraged toward a desired destination but all too frequently are not told exactly how to get there. For example, men are exhorted to be the spiritual leader in the family and marriage but not told how to make it happen. Women are encouraged to submit to their husbands, but no one explains how to process the troublesome issues of their hearts. Well-meaning, biblical exhortations that lack explanation can easily lead to frustration, guilt, and perhaps even despair. It seems we need a map app, not just a compass.

That's why we want to give you the map app approach to marital intimacy. Marriage relationships are all over the map, so to speak. Husbands and wives need to come to grips with their current location and think seriously about their desired destination of a more satisfying spiritual and emotional connection.

PRAY TOGETHER

> *For where two or three gather in my name, there am I with them.*
>
> —MATTHEW 18:20

⤳ *Father, we thank You for our marriage and for our relationship with You. We believe You have created marriage as the relationship between a man and a woman, and we believe marriage is the engine of the home and family. Your will is for our marriage to be the most personal and highest priority relationship for each of us as husband and wife, out-side of our relationships with You. Marriage is the most intimate gath-ering of two in Your name, and we are confident that as we are married in Your name, You are here with us, day by day, moment by moment. Amen.*

A THREE-STRAND CORD

I was so grateful to hear your message—your testimony was deeply convicting to me. You see, through your talk, God showed me that I had not been leading my family, most especially my wife, in the way He would have me to do. After the conference, I went home and shared your story with her. Then I apologized to my wife, and we talked through some of the issues in our family. Now we have committed to praying together every day; it has been wonderful for our marriage. I look forward to passing this along to the many married men at my church. I'll let you know how it goes.

—JOHN

After speaking to you on Sunday, I feel a new sense of purpose in my marriage and my walk with Christ. Paula and I had our first prayertime together yesterday, which was more spontaneous than planned, but I initiated it and led. As we held hands and prayed, I could feel the Holy Spirit upon us. We look forward to more time together and the hope of more blessing in our marriage and our family.

—RICK

A cord of three strands is not quickly broken.

—ECCLESIASTES 4:12

God's map app for spiritual growth in your marriage consists of three parts: the marriage itself, the Bible, and prayer. When all work together, your way to the destination of intimacy and spiritual well-being is assured.

MARRIAGE, THE STARTING POINT

Obviously, you must be married in order to grow in intimacy with a spouse. For most of human history, the definition of marriage was also considered evident, but more recently, people have tried to obscure the obvious. So just to clarify: we believe marriage is God's institution as revealed in the Bible, a unique and committed relationship between one man and one woman who have covenanted before God to live together for the entirety of their earthly lives. Marriage is an exclusive, intimate relationship and is the core of the home and family. And it is an intimate relationship in every aspect of life's journey.

This exclusivity and uniqueness is first demonstrated in the creation story. The wonder of God's creation across the heavens and earth was beyond glorious. God Himself affirmed "it is good" over every result of His creative hand. Yet something was lacking, perhaps not quite completely good. To be specific: *someone* was missing. Adam, who was designed for relationship by the breath of God, did not have a suitable companion. Although God paraded the animal kingdom before Adam, there was not a helper suitable for him, and Adam was keenly aware of his aloneness. God, of course, knew of the problem and explained to Adam (and us) his need: "It is not good for the man to be alone. I will make a helper suitable for him" (Genesis 2:18).

The Great Physician put Adam into a deep sleep and removed a rib from Adam's side. The rib became the source material for fashioning Eve. In that Eve was God's final creative work, you might even say that she is the crowning creation. Scripture specifically says she is the perfect companion-helper who completes the image of God in Adam: "So God created mankind in his own image, in the image of God he created them; male and female He created them" (Genesis 1:26).

God brought Eve to Adam for the most unique relationship he would experience on earth. Loneliness was vanquished:

> *For this reason a man shall leave his father and his mother,*
> *and be joined to his wife; and they shall become one flesh.*
> *And the man and his wife were both naked and were not*
> *ashamed.*
>
> —GENESIS 2:24–25 NASB

Not only is marriage the heart of the family, it is the foundational relationship of society, the union that provides the proper context for procreation, and the umbrella of provision and protection needed by every successive generation.

WORD OF GOD, THE REFERENCE POINT

The Bible is no ordinary book. It is the inspired Word of God from cover to cover. It is "living and powerful, and sharper than any two-edged sword, piercing even to the division of soul and spirit, and of joints and marrow, and is a discerner of the thoughts and intents of the heart" (Hebrews 4:12 NKJV). Yet some people approach the Bible like a magic book that will help them acquire whatever they want in life. But that is, emphatically, not its purpose. The Word of God has the ability to penetrate the souls of men and women. It can speak to our hearts, discerning our thoughts and even our motives. Using Scripture, the Holy Spirit can guide, convict, convince, and teach us in the intimacy of our personal reading and meditation. As we develop intimacy with Christ individually through God's Word, the overflow of our relationship with Him can't help but bless our marriages, something that we'll discuss more fully together here.

PRAYER, THE TRANSMISSION SIGNAL

A story emerged on the Internet (so it must be true, right?) about a bar that needed to expand its building. In response, a nearby church struck up a campaign of petition and prayer meetings to block the bar's expansion. Nevertheless, local authorities approved the necessary building permits and construction moved forward. About a week before the grand reopening, a massive thunderstorm arose and a bolt of lightning struck the bar and burned it to the ground.

As a result of this "act of God," the church members grew a bit smug, bragging about the power of prayer. The angry bar owner, in turn, sued the church on grounds that it was "ultimately responsible for the demise of the building, through direct actions or indirect means," but the church vehemently denied all responsibility or any connection to the building's demise. After carefully reading through the plaintiff's (bar owner) complaint and the defendant's (church) reply, the judge opened the legal proceedings by saying, "I don't know how I am going to decide this case, but it appears from the paperwork before me that what we have here is a bar owner who now believes in the power of prayer and an entire church that does not!" I don't know who won the case, but the judge's point is well taken. Prayer makes a difference in life.

Prayer is communicating with God, connecting with Him in a way that we believe can change things in and around our lives. The Bible tells us that God is *transcendent*—majestic, beyond all that we can imagine, and utterly holy—set apart. God lives in "unapproachable light" (1 Timothy 6:16), and no man can see His face. Throughout Scripture God tells us that seeing Him is so glorious and majestic that man would not be able to handle it; it would kill mere mortals. (For example, in Exodus 33, God hides Moses in the cleft of a rock while His glory passes by because He knows Moses wouldn't be able to see His glory and live.) Because man is naturally unholy, apart from the person of Christ, we have no chance to commune with God, let alone see Him. God is utterly holy and set apart from man. Yet, God is also immensely personal. He knows every hair on our heads, every thought and intention of our hearts, and He still loves us! The One who knows you the best, loves you the most.

If you knew everything about us, you might decide you don't care for us very much. Yet God, rather than being repulsed and rejecting us as sinners, calls believers in Jesus Christ His friends! And He offers this friendship to everyone. Through the intimacy of personally connecting with God in prayer, people can have communion with God, and the more we connect with Him, the more we become like Him. As 2 Corinthians 3:17–18 says:

> Now the Lord is the Spirit, and where the Spirit of the Lord is, there is freedom. And we all, who with unveiled faces contemplate the Lord's glory, are being transformed into his image with every-increasing glory, which comes from the Lord, who is the Spirit.

PUTTING THE CORD TOGETHER

So, marriage, Scripture, and prayer—God is the author and provider of all three. Spinning together these three sources of strength from God creates a powerful cord. But spiritual intimacy in many marriages is lacking. In particular, husbands and wives do not pray together very much. We may have routine prayertimes over meals or in a small groups, but making the opportunity to come before God's throne of grace as husband and wife is often deficient in most homes. We know that this gap is not due to a lack of desire. It's just that most of us simply don't know what to do to improve spiritual connectivity in our marriages.

The answer, though, is closer at hand than most would imagine. The Bible is the most excellent guide for our prayers. The Holy Spirit will show up in our marriages through His Word and will show us what He wants us to pray together. Through praying Scripture, our prayers can become as fresh as the flow of God's Word itself!

For too many years, we missed the connection by holding the three strands separately from one another. We prayed and studied Scripture individually but not together. When we became intentional about weaving together the separate strands of our marriage, everything in our marriage, family, and ministry changed. You can make this adjustment as well. That is exactly why we believe God led you pick up this book.

PRAY TOGETHER

Unless the LORD *builds the house, the builders labor in vain. Unless the* LORD *watches over the city, the guards stand watch in vain.*

—PSALM 127:1–2

⌐→ *Lord, when Solomon wrote this declaration, it appears that he was primarily referring to the building of Your house, the Temple of God. But we see that the principle applies to our marriage as well. So we ask You to be the Builder of our marriage and family. We petition You to watch over our home. Our heart is to avoid the vain efforts of trying to build and watch on our own. You are Lord! Amen.*

OUR GREAT
AWAKENING

I was able to identify with some of the same issues that Sam described, and at one point, I was overwhelmed with the sense that this is what I need to be doing with my wife. Since then, Sandy and I have been simply praying the Word, and it has been good. There seems to be the power of "two or more gathered together" in our praying, and it certainly has brought us closer together along with rein-forcing my role as pastor of my family.

—GREG

Thank you for sharing your marriage experience and the Lord's Word He has revealed to you. My wife and I have learned so much! We started to read the Bible together and pray God's Word. We decided to start with the Book of Ephesians. We are having great time together. I accept the challenge to encourage other Christian men to pray with their wives. It is transforming my marriage, and I know will do the same for others also.

—PASTOR ALEXANDER

*I*n this house we do second chances; we do real; we do grace; we do mistakes; we do I'm sorry; we do hugs; we do family; we do love.

A plaque hanging on the wall in our den announces these core family values. And trust us: we've had plenty of chances over the years to work on living it out. We have come to know that grace is the glue of relationships—with God, in marriage, among parents and children, between siblings, and with others outside the family. Frankly, we know of no other effective way to push through the muddy patches of life. Everyone is going to stumble at some point. Disappoint. Fail. Mess up. *Sin.*

TOGETHER AGAIN

We believe God is a specialist in restoration. The mistakes, failures, sufferings, and even our sins become the custom building blocks of our lives. This is what Paul tells us in Romans 8:28: "And we know that in all things God works for the good of those who love him, who have been called according to his purpose."

When we think of the holiness of God, our first reaction is to think He is severely repulsed by sin. Certainly, sin separates from God and condemns us before Him—this is accurate theology—but be careful, because it does not end there. While we are sinners by nature, attitude, and actions, God hates our sin, but He absolutely loves the sinner. Romans 5:6–8 is clear about this:

> *You see, at just the right time, when we were still powerless, Christ died for the ungodly. Very rarely will anyone die for a righteous person, though for a good person someone might possibly dare to die. But God demonstrates his own love for us in this: While we were still sinners, Christ died for us.*

And that's not all. Paul continues, laying it on even heavier, lest we miss the sublime truth:

> *Since we have now been justified by his blood, how much more shall we be saved from God's wrath through him! For if, while we were God's enemies, we were reconciled to him through the death of his Son, how much more, having been reconciled, shall we be saved through his life! Not only is this so, but we also boast in God through our Lord Jesus Christ, through whom we have now received reconciliation.*
>
> —ROMANS 5:9–11

God is a God of reconciliation! He seeks to convert His enemies into His children. This transaction was neither casual nor simple from God's perspective. His justice required payment for the sins we, His enemies, committed, but His love would sacrifice His Son Jesus to make this reconciliation possible. Through our faith in Jesus Christ, we rejoice as sons and daughters of God who are held secure in His hands. This is the rock foundation of the gospel, which we hold as the most basic confession of our faith. The reconciling love of God not only brings believers in Christ through the narrow gate of God's kingdom but also carries us on the journey of the narrow way through the ups and downs of our lives.

What does this mean? It means the prodigal can come home. When we sin, we have an Advocate. If we are being swept along in the broad way that leads to destruction, God can rescue us from the swift and swirling current. Broken pieces can be gathered and assembled. The offender and offended can be reconciled. The guilty can be forgiven. Light illuminates dark places. It even means God can restore what may have been lost along the way.

God extends grace to us from the beginning of our walk with Him and on through the whole journey. And His mercy is for us to share. God not only wants to give good things *to* us but to channel them *through* us. The grace we receive is not for us to keep all to ourselves. It is to be shared with others. This sharing, though, can be the hard part. We have been hurt, disappointed, betrayed, disillusioned, and maybe even lied to. We may not have felt much grace from other people, so we need to call upon God to fill us with His grace in order that, through us, He can extend it to those around us.

Much of our story is about how this grace came into our marriage when we needed it most. Allow us to share how this played out.

THE PRODIGAL DAUGHTER

The day after Easter in March 2008, our family saw a phenomenal miracle of God. Our first daughter, Christina, had wandered from the Lord into the broad way that leads to destruction (Matthew 7:13-14 NKJV). This wayward journey encompassed a substantial portion of her late teens, carried on through college, and stretched into her young adult years.

We earnestly sought to raise our three daughters the best we knew how and to pour Christ into them. We went to church regularly. In fact, Sam was an associate pastor! Our children went to Sunday School, youth group, summer camp—the whole nine yards.

You may know what we're talking about. Perhaps you have done some "broad way" time in your own life. Or maybe you are suffering right now through the antics of a wayward child. You've done all you know to do as a Christian parent. You tried to be sufficient role models as a believer in Jesus Christ, but *still*, the reality is that our kids and grandkids ultimately need to "own their own faith."

Just as it was with each of us when we were young, our children learn the most about really assimilating faith in the Lord by encountering troubles. Some people seem to need to "taste blood, sweat, and tears" to take ownership of their faith, and the broad way is very good at delivering on that need. For a complex set of reasons, Christina ended up in a really bad place. She never actually renounced Jesus Christ, but she wandered very far from Him.

Then, one wonderful day in 2008, Christina dramatically returned to the Lord in profound repentance. God broke into the center of her attention and moved powerfully in her heart. She truly surrendered to Him and embarked upon what has become a complete transformation of her life. Now she is seriously seeking to walk with God.

A dear friend of ours, who saw God's victory in the life of his wayward son, said to us, "When these kids go out there, far from God, and then He brings them back, they don't come back normal; they come back warriors!" That exactly describes what God did for Christina, and we are deeply grateful for His marvelous miracle of grace in our family.

Let us also declare to you the wondrous truth that we told Christina the night she came home: God can "repay you for the years the locusts have eaten" (Joel 2:25). We also told her that if she would fix her attention on the Lord, and draw near to God, He would draw near to her (James 4:7-8). And that God could fast track her healing and growth. In fact, He restored her to where she would have been in spiritual maturity—perhaps even surpassing that place—specifically because she had been to hell and back. God did not waste anything!

We wish we could tell you we fought faithfully in prayer for Christina during those wayward years. Sure, we prayed for her but, honestly, not as we should have. Yet God even used our failure to bring transformation and fruit. He uses everything in our lives to teach us and to put a rock foundation under our feet. We praise God for this grace! And in particular, for the reconciliation He sealed into Christina's life and into our family. Truly, the experience of this long trial in our family became one of the building blocks to create this book.

How?

YOU HAVE FAILED ME

A fair label you could post on every marriage is "under construction." Maintaining unity in marriage is like shooting at a moving target, largely because the stages of life continuously face us with fresh challenges like:

* newlywed adjustments;
* caring for babies and young children (24/7!);
* potentially facing the trials of infertility;
* finding balance in raising teenagers;
* managing college years and the attendant costs;
* ups and downs of aging and health;
* uncertain financial conditions;
* instability with employment during insecure economic times;
* geographic moves;
* handling trials, troubles, and temptations;
* attending to aging and ailing parents;
* and on and on.

Life is real, difficult, and challenging!

We are closing in on our fortieth wedding anniversary, and in a way, we have no idea where all those years have gone. Since coming to personal faith in Jesus Christ at the same time during our college days, we have journeyed the Christian life together. We have long sought to have a Christ-centered marriage. Yet the "under construction" facet means that our three-way bond with God is an ongoing and *on-growing* relationship in progress.

Being under construction brought us to our encounter with *the* question—a fateful date in God's providence we both remember well. We had run into a rough patch in our marriage. A number of issues bubbled around, churning up stress and tension. The difficulties affected many aspects of our lives and marriage, and things got rather confusing.

Reflecting on our situation brings to mind a simple analogy to what we were going through. Sam loves bass fishing and is a fairly decent fisherman, but sometimes a poor cast will "backlash" and create a bird's nest of tangled fishing line. When that happens, as any fisherman knows, you are done fishing for a while. Untangling that wadded mess is a frustrating and time-consuming chore.

In our stressful season, our marriage line had backlashed. More than once, we sat in the living room and talked for hours, attempting to work through what was happening to us. We tried to figure out "Just what in the world is going on?" Finally, during one of our talks, an unsettling reality emerged from Vicki's heart.

"You know what Sam," she said, "part of what is going on here is that I am feeling like . . . *you have failed me.*"

The words rocked our world. They were far from normal for Vicki. Four powerful, penetrating words: "You have failed me." Each one was an incoming rocket!

Vicki's admission did not arise from long-standing bitterness but from a realization that finally came to light for her. She went on to say, "You failed me because, during Christina's long journey in the broad way, you did not pray with me to consistently fight for her soul over those years. I largely felt like I had to do it on my own."

This does not mean we never prayed together for our daughter, but it does mean Sam, as the husband and father, had not provided the spiritual leadership and initiative in our marriage to consistently pray for our wayward daughter. We should have been far more intentional and regular with the weapon of prayer to fight for Christina's soul. Vicki was dead right!

At the core of the rough patch was the painful reality that our girls faced a number of serious issues in their lives. Vicki was burdened that, as their parents, we needed to pray together about those matters. Furthermore, Vicki continued, "I am emotionally tired and worn out. I just cannot do this alone anymore."

But even that wasn't all.

"Sam," she said, "beyond praying for our daughters, the fact is I need to connect more with you *spiritually*."

Vicki was right. We needed to share spiritual life together. To a degree we were, but, looking back, we would describe our spiritual lives as "haphazardly touching." We orbited here and there into spiritual connectedness, and although we would go to church regularly, pray at meals, talk about a sermon we heard, and share spiritual insights, our interaction lacked purpose and initiative. The missing piece was the consistent, intentional connection of praying together. The lack of spiritual oneness was a burden for both of us.

THE REVELATION AWAITS

The Old Testament prophet Habakkuk complained a lot to God. He thought God should show up and sort out all the foolishness and sin, which was rampant among His people. The whining continued until God finally shocked Habakkuk by announcing that He was preparing the Babylonians to bring a judgment upon the Israelites. In Habakkuk 2:3, God explained the timing: "For the revelation awaits an appointed time; it speaks of the end and will not prove false. Though it linger, wait for it; it will certainly come and will not delay."

Did you catch that line: "for the revelation awaits an appointed time"? This verse is about the sovereignty of God. In *His* timing, God reveals what will happen.

When the light flicks on in our lives, it is not usually because we learn new information. Often, we already have the information, and what we need is the revelation of how the Lord awakens us and gains our attention through a particular event or season of life. In the mystery of God's sovereignty, the revelation comes about at His "appointed time."

Sometimes we think God's timing is pretty bad, don't we? But we are not God, and frequently, only God understands the reasons for His timing. On occasion, we get a glimpse of the "why," but often, we are in the dark. Waiting is a call for us to trust Him.

GUILTY AS CHARGED

In reality, the confrontation that day was not from Vicki; it was from the Lord. As all of the accusation and hurt tumbled out of Vicki's heart, Sam literally lifted up his hands, as if under arrest, and said, "Guilty . . . guilty!" He recognized the revelation of God and His timing. The conviction of God fell heavy, and appropriately so.

The all-is-not-right feelings we'd been having were an alarm clock ringing, trying to wake us—especially Sam—to our need for spiritual connection. But we—especially Sam, again—kept hitting the snooze button, just so we could move on with life. Finally, the alarm rang with enough force and volume that hitting the snooze button was no longer an option.

Sam was broken and confessed, "It hardly seems sufficient to cover the scope of what we are talking about here, but I want to tell you: I am sorry. With all my heart, I am *so* sorry!"

NEVER AGAIN

It's a wonderful thing to perceive the grace of God. As the revelation of conviction and repentance fell simultaneously, Sam embraced a firm resolve.

"You know what, Vicki?" he announced, "By the grace of God, I promise this is not going to happen again!"

His words carried the weight of the vows we had exchanged at the wedding altar years before.

"The best we can, within the reasonable limitations and realities of life, we are going to pray together," he proclaimed. "I know life is very busy, unpredictable, a moving target, but daily prayer together will be the goal. And I am going to take the lead in initiating. I vow to be intentional."

SAYING THE WORD

Two gifts from God fell in our living room that afternoon. One was a gift of repentance, and the other was a gift of revelation. The Lord instantly showed us *how* we were going to make this work.

Sam sensed God speaking to his heart: "Sam, pray *My Word* with Vicki." That was our solution! That would be the path we could follow forward. We decided to pray the Bible. We would let Scripture be the guide—the template—for our prayers. We decided to intentionally follow God's Word in our prayers. We would do "Scripture praying."

Sam continued, "We'll read a paragraph of the Bible together, see how the Holy Spirit speaks to our hearts, and then we will let the text of the Bible be the guide for what we will pray back to God. We'll run on the tracks of the Scriptures to give us the ideas and content for our prayers. Then we'll pray about a few of the other things that are immediately at hand in our lives—family and ministry—and that's it. We'll keep it short, and then be on our way."

And you know what? It was awesome!

NOT SPIRITUAL ENOUGH

Often, we don't feel creative enough or spiritual enough to pray with the same person every day or regularly. We're not sure how to sweep the heavens with just the right "thees," "thous," spiritual insights, and discerning intercessions. We know we'll likely end up praying every time about essentially the same things in the same way. We're afraid we'll bore our prayer partner, ourselves, or maybe even God!

But by following the Word of God and by letting the Bible supply the text of our prayers, God will take care of keeping the prayers fresh. We will become as creative and comprehensive as the Bible itself! What's more, we will be praying "on target"—the Word and will of God over our lives, families, and ministries—in an ever fresh and empowered manner. With the Bible as prayer book, you can't miss praying in and for God's will.

PRAY TOGETHER

Therefore, since we have a great high priest who has ascended into heaven, Jesus the Son of God, let us hold firmly to the faith we profess. For we do not have a high priest who is unable to empathize with our weaknesses, but we have one who has been tempted in every way, just as we are—yet he did not sin. Let us then approach God's throne of grace with confidence, so that we may receive mercy and find grace to help us in our time of need.

—HEBREWS 4:14–16

Lord, we are comforted to know that You understand and empathize with our weaknesses. We are blessed with the confidence that Jesus has gone to heaven before us as our great High Priest and that we are able to come before Your throne together. We thank You that Your throne is characterized by grace so we can come boldly before You. We do not have to be hesitant or fearful—no matter what troubles or issues we have in our lives—because Jesus has gone before us, and He opens the way as our great High Priest. Amen!

DESIGNED TO CARRY AND WAIT

*Since I wrote to you almost two years ago, my husband
Dave and I have continued praying and reading Scripture
together. We have read and prayed through many books
in the New Testament and have recently started the Book
of Matthew. God is so faithful as He continues to grow
us closer to each other as a couple, and most importantly
closer to Him. Neither of us ever dreamed we would be
able to read Scripture and pray out loud with each other.
I personally thank you and praise God that He is using
this message to "advance His kingdom" in a middle-aged
couple in Iowa. Glory to God!*

—DAWN

God uniquely designed the woman's body to carry and give
birth to children. It is a divine privilege, as well as an awesome
responsibility.

Sometimes women say they are "not ready for children," but I
(Vicki) suggest we are rarely ready to do many of the things God calls
us to do. Even so, He providentially brings many things into our lives
with the intention of developing us, step by step along the journey.

CHAPTER 4

IN TRANSITION

Some years ago, I stood before my bathroom mirror. Beholding my reflection, I uttered a desperate prayer to God: *I am really weary of waiting for my husband to understand that I have a need for him to pray with me. I am normally the one who initiates or suggests, "Can we pray about this or that issue." I feel like I am begging him to do something that he should be doing! Why is it always like this? How long do I need to wait? It seems like he is asleep at the wheel. After all, isn't that part of being the head of our home? I am starting to doubt this will ever happen in our marriage. I am beginning to resent him, and I confess I am also mad at You, God.*

Soon after that prayer I realized I was spiritually "in transition."

In childbirth terminology, transition is defined as the phase of labor just before the baby is born. In transition, the pain and pressure reach their peak. In giving birth to our three daughters, the transition phase of my labor varied from several minutes to two hours. Compared to some women who have far longer transition periods, I suppose I was lucky. But no matter how long it lasts, transition is no fun!

Standing before the mirror that day, I felt like I had been carrying something in the spiritual realm for years. Doubt overwhelmed any hope that whatever it was would ever be birthed into reality, and I placed the blame squarely on my husband and God.

Even though I poured out my heart before the Lord, I still felt so full of emotion that I could burst. Yet God was about to give me an important insight. I just needed to stop ranting long enough to listen.

I sometimes question whether or not God is speaking to me, but when I think I hear something that I could not possibly come up with on my most creative day, I know it is from Him. So, as I paused after my ravings that day, my spirit heard something my mind will never forget, and the insight set me on a new path. It even enabled me to pass through that particular transition phase with God's perspective. Here's what I believe God showed me about my circumstances that day: *When I created Eve, I put Adam to sleep. When I am finished fashioning you, Vicki, I will wake Sam up!*

Although I have never been struck by lightning, the impact of these intimate words from the Lord electrified me. The effect was energizing, intense, life-changing, and illuminating. It was my burning bush, my Damascus road—God had my attention!

OVERWAIT, UNDERWAIT, OR JUST RIGHT?

After 40 long years, it is easy to imagine Moses might give up on any idea that he could help deliver the Hebrews from the Egyptians. But when God was ready—at just the right time—the wait was over. God spoke to Moses through the bush that burned with fire without being consumed. The Lord's message enabled Moses to do extraordinary things because he knew God was now going to take over. Any humanly impossible task can only be fulfilled through the touch of our supernatural God.

Like Moses facing the burning bush, God spoke truth to me the day I faced myself in the mirror, and He gave me fresh hope. For years, the desire for my husband to pray with me distracted my attention from the broader purpose of God's timing and power. My focus bounced between my husband's failure and my disappointment. Sure, I had times when I would rehearse God's faithfulness in answering my prayers, but mostly, I had lost my emotional stability, and I stayed angry and frustrated as a result of trying to stabilize my feelings in my own power.

No one could really see the turmoil inside of me, yet at times it spilled out in harsh looks and words of criticism. You know what they say: "If momma ain't happy, ain't nobody happy!" Like it or not, as married women, we are the thermostats of our homes. God designed this womanly influence to be a constructive force in the marriage and family. When we are warm and settled, all is well. But when we are fraught with resentment and disappointments, things can go pretty cold.

When God spoke to my heart that day, I wondered how long I would have to wait for my heart's desire to come true. He was refocusing the vision of my heart on a big-picture perspective, and I needed to see what He would do. Since the timing hadn't worked out to my satisfaction yet, I realized that He was still adding some finishing touches to *me*. This is not to say that the issue was just about me and that I was the only problem. But God awakened a realization that He knew exactly where both my husband and I were at that time—and that He was still working on me in this painful transition phase. He merely sought my cooperation and patience for His timing to play out.

Moses learned the hard way that God was in control of all timing. Forty years in the desert is a long time. Although I hadn't been in my desert that long, my hope tank was nearing the empty mark. But thanks to God's "just right" timing and my new perspective on His work, my tank started refilling.

PUT HER IN THE BASKET

Another thought came to me in those moments at the mirror. God rewound my memory to a lesson He taught me years before: waiting also involves letting go.

I recalled when Christina was 18 and going through the difficult season we described in the previous chapter. She was walking in the broad way that leads to destruction, as Jesus describes it, and as a result of her problems, I was not doing so well myself. Anxiety was crushing me.

As part of our ministry with e3 Partners Ministry, Sam and I were scheduled to lead a short-term missions trip to Romania, but I felt that if I left the country—even though it was for only a week— I would be abandoning Christina. My staying behind would not have helped her, but I was still terrified to leave the country.

One sleepless night before our departure, I was wrestling with my own emotions—and with the Lord. The predawn hours found me in our backyard, wringing my hands as I paced and prayed near our small pool.

"I just can't do this, Lord. If You don't give me some peace about this trip, I am not going to leave my daughter!"

I stopped pacing and felt silence envelope me. Five simple words whispered in my heart: "Put her in the basket."

By faith, Moses's mother placed her three-month-old baby boy in a papyrus basket coated with tar and pitch and set him among the reeds of the Nile River. God was symbolically prompting me to do likewise with Christina. I needed to put her in God's "basket" and let Him take care of her.

Moses's mother had no idea how her son's story would end. Certainly she could not have imagined who her son would become and how he would be anointed by God to lead Israel's great Exodus from Egypt through the parted Red Sea! All she could do was to obey God's instructions. She had to have been a woman of great faith. The papyrus basket represented the hands, heart, and providence of her God. No matter what creatures or currents might threaten in the

Nile River, she placed baby Moses in the best place possible: into God's care.

Could I have followed those instructions? Could I release a helpless, dependent infant into a hostile environment and trust that God would watch over him? My daughter was no infant, but her environment was as hostile as any I cared to think about. Yet, God challenged me to let go, to trust Him by an act of will that would hopefully convince my heart to follow.

I symbolically placed my daughter into the care of her heavenly Father and released her from the care of her earthly mother. Peace came over me, and I knew the Lord had given me the grace to follow His direction. The peace freed me to enjoy the missions trip, but more importantly, it continued through a long, dark time for Christina. Although there were ups and downs over the years ahead, the experience with God that night gave me a benchmark I could refer to and remember my commitment: that I put her in the basket.

In both the backyard concerning Christina and at the mirror regarding Sam, God wanted me to refocus and release—refocus on His timing and promises, and release my desires to His faithfulness and purpose. From transition to birth took about ten years, and, trust me, it was not smooth sailing all the way, but reading about God's fashioning of Eve during Adam's anesthesia, changed the direction of my focus and the content of my prayers for my husband.

GETTING OUT FROM BETWEEN YOUR HUSBAND AND GOD

As God shined the spotlight on me, I remembered something He showed me years earlier that I had forgotten and utterly failed to put into practice. It happened one other time when I had been pointing the finger at (what I considered) Sam's shortcomings.

My thinking had been greatly affected by a problem I've discovered from speaking to numerous women over the years. It seems we share a common weakness. In fact, it's more than just a weakness. It's a *curse*.

After Adam and Eve disobeyed God's prohibition of eating from the tree of knowledge of good and evil, God meted out a two-fold consequence to Eve, as recorded in Genesis 3:16: (1) pain in childbearing and (2) desire for her husband. We can easily understand the first consequence, but the second one can be a bit confusing. A mentor of mine counseled me about this verse some years ago. She shared with me that the "desire for your husband" was not of a sexual, physical nature, but was a desire for authority—for ruling over him! So women are cursed with the proclivity to seek dominion over their husbands.

I have struggled with this and have seen other women of all age ranges, cultures, and contexts struggle with it as well. We have a predisposition, an innate pull, a natural tendency to want to tell our husbands what to do—to "mother them," if you will. In fact, doing this is often our first response in situations of home and marriage.

I was pulled into the vortex of that Evelike desire. Not only was I trying to tell my husband how to shape up, sometimes I attempted to run the universe by advising God on when and what needed doing. When I finally came to my senses, I saw myself standing between God and Sam, pointing fingers at each of them. I decided a better posture would be for me to get out from in between and get onto my knees. I needed to let the problem be between God and Sam directly.

God used this period of waiting to fashion *my* character, my words, my heart, and my vision! He freed me to pray and wait with a different perspective on Sam because I had released him into God's hands. I no longer prayed that Sam would "get it" and relieve what I selfishly viewed as my misery. Instead, while praying, I would envision myself on my knees, out of the way, giving God permission to fashion *me*. I let God work on me until He decided to wake up my husband.

SUNLIGHT VERSUS MOONLIGHT

Sunlight and moonlight have the same source but yield drastically different results. Enormous chemical reactions within the sun generate light that beams through nearly 93 million miles of space where it radiates toward our planet, causing growth in the plant kingdom. The moon, on the other hand, is merely a satellite of earth and does not generate its own light. The source of its light is the sun, but the light is only *reflected* from the sun and cannot produce growth. If you have any doubts, try an experiment with two plants. Place one outdoors or in a window where it can receive ample sunlight each day. Place the other plant in a dark closet, and bring it out only during the night to bask in moonlight. And what happens? It's a no-brainer, really. Light from the sun is direct from the source and contains the power to grow life, but moonlight, reflected from the sun, has no power to nurture living things. Similarly, people can experience these two sorts of "light" from God.

As Saul was on a journey to Damascus (see Acts 9) to further his project of persecuting those who claimed the name of Jesus Christ, a bright light flashed all around him. He fell to the ground and heard a voice say, in verses 4 and 5, "Saul, Saul, why do you persecute me?"

"Who are you, Lord?" Saul asked.

"I am Jesus, whom you are persecuting."

Saul did not recognize the voice of Jesus because he had never heard it for himself. His information about who Jesus was and what He came to do was based solely upon what religious leaders had said about Jesus. They were as spiritually blind as Saul became physically blinded by the great light that appeared before him on the road to Damascus. Not until Jesus appeared and gave Saul the direct light of His presence did Saul know who Jesus really was.

When Jesus walked the earth, He had various instructions for the people He met:

* "Follow me" (Matthew 4:19-20).
* "Come . . . and learn from me" (Matthew 11:28-30).
* "My sheep listen to my voice; I know them, and they follow me" (John 10:27-28).
* A commendation for Mary who sat at Jesus' feet listening to His words (Luke 10:38-42).

Jesus Christ is the direct light of God. He instructs us to soak in the rays of His truth and love in order to grow. Certainly, God can direct His light to us through other sources—sermons, books, tapes, radio and television broadcasts, articles on the Internet, friends and mentors—but we need to ask ourselves: what is our default source for light from God? Jesus told one follower in Luke 10:41-42, "Martha, Martha, . . . you are worried and upset about many things, but few things are needed—or indeed only one. Mary has chosen what is better, and it will not be taken away from her" (Mary had chosen Jesus' light).

In troubled times, my first response for many years was to pick up the phone, grab a book, or search for a candy bar. While there are worse things to grab, often I wanted what I thought would bring the quickest relief. I did not want to sit still, wait, and pray in His presence. I didn't look straight to the Son-light for help. I am not trying to wax unrealistic or over spiritual because I continue to be challenged in my life. I am talking about genuine pursuit of God. The question for each of us is: do I gravitate toward books, sermons, and friends for help, or do I turn straight to the Source? As I have developed the discipline to turn my face toward the Son, my growth has been more consistent, His voice has been clearer, and my path has been brighter.

Saul was struck blind in his encounter with the Son and forced to wait in darkness for a time. While we may not be apostles, we are wives, mothers, and grandmothers—individual women of God who can change our own worlds. As we still ourselves in Jesus' presence, the Son-light we receive will help us grow up. This stable growth from the Lord will enable us to wait, pray, and trust as God's sovereign hand fashions us into more of His image—even through a long, painful transition phase!

It is rather common among women in the torture of the transition phase of childbirth to want to quit. *What am I doing here?* They think. *I am outta here! I am just going to get off of this table and forget it, because this birth is not going to happen!* But that's crazy, right? We simply don't have that choice. Instead, we have to wait for it to pass.

IN THE WAITING ROOM

It seems we spend much of our lives in waiting rooms. By the nature and through the process of doing life, we wait for the next need, desire, result, or outcome. You might want to start a family, launch a career, improve your finances, get through some medical tests, make it to the end of the semester, go on vacation, or to have the holidays come or go. Wait. Wait. Wait. Maybe you're waiting—like I was—for your husband to wake up from his sleep and pray with you . . . at his initiative. Meanwhile, you don't see any movement.

After summoning Jesus to come heal their dying brother (John 11), Mary and Martha saw no movement for three days. They were waiting for the solution they thought best: Jesus needed to get to their house soon enough to heal Lazarus so he wouldn't die. I imagine if they gazed out the window once, they gazed out the window a hundred times waiting for Jesus to come. All the while, they had no control of the timing, the outcome, or the broader purposes of Jesus, which they did not understand. The only thing they had control over was themselves. What were they doing for those three days besides looking out the window? Complaining? Worrying? Praying? Perhaps all of those? What do we do in the waiting rooms of our lives? There are many possibilities, but one thing I know for sure is that we should avoid the what-ifs.

Nothing tortures the human soul as much as contemplating the what-ifs. What if he doesn't get the job? What if she doesn't get that scholarship? What if the tests come back positive? What if my circumstances never change, and I am stuck in this waiting room forever? For Mary and Martha, it was: what if Lazarus dies?

They had a lot riding on Lazarus's health and well-being. Since they were single women for whom the dream of marriage was not yet fulfilled, they likely depended on brother Lazarus for their livelihood and security. Their ultimate what-if was, "What if he dies and we are left without him?" This legitimate fear be devastating, enough to send them into a pit of despair. The what-ifs abound in every direction our soul can run, and they cannot be controlled. The truth is that our most-feared what-ifs almost never come to pass, but even if they do—like for Mary and Martha—God still has a way out.

We need to guard our minds and hearts from the what-ifs. They are not from the Lord and are likely energized in our souls by the enemy. Satan wants to distract our minds with things we cannot control, so that the thing we can control is neglected. Remember, Jesus cautioned Martha of this very thing: "You are worried and upset about many things, but few things are needed—or indeed only one" (Luke 10:41-42). Jesus said, *Only one* thing is needed! In the waiting rooms of life, we should not neglect that one thing. It's the only thing we have surefire control over while we are waiting: to sit at Jesus' feet seeking His face, love, Word, and perspective.

ALL I NEED IS YOU

An idol can be a tricky thing. I wonder if Lazarus may have become somewhat of an idol for Mary and Martha because of their dependence upon him as the man in their lives. I suspect that, as Jesus delayed coming, He was allowing them to reprioritize their lives. It is difficult to detect that someone or something is an idol in our lives until it is changed or removed. Our children, jobs, creature comforts, even our husbands, could become an idol if we place an exaggerated dependency upon them. Their importance can replace the priority and primacy of a personal relationship with God. I wonder if Jesus was requiring Mary and Martha to reevaluate Lazarus's position in their lives and come back to the basic words of Jesus, that one thing—a personal relationship with Him—is necessary!

God challenged me on the importance I had placed on my husband changing in this one area of praying with me. God showed that it was consuming me and hindering my faith relationship and trust of Him. Could I accept that perhaps I had to live without my husband ever initiating prayer with me? Could I believe that Jesus was really all I needed? Is Jesus Christ truly the primary Vine of which I am a branch to bear fruit? Was a lack in my husband becoming a reason to justify my own lagging relationship with God? I thought God's delay represented His lack of care until I realized that His delay in changing Sam was precisely the best thing He could do to help my most important relationship—with God.

OVERCOME BY OUR TESTIMONIES

Every person who places his or her personal faith in Jesus Christ has a story of how he or she learned about Jesus' death and Resurrection. Often we call this our personal testimony. We reflect on the moment when God convicted us of our sin and gave us the revelation that Jesus offers forgiveness based on His shed blood. That's when we are born again into God's family through childlike trust in this truth. But such a one-time testimony is not the only testimony we have to offer. We also have an ongoing testimony: the story of how God continues to reveal Himself and His kingdom truths to us over time. Sharing these testimonies with each other is also a source of encouragement and revelation.

As they waited for Jesus, Mary and Martha did not know God was about to give them one of the greatest testimonies in history. Their testimony—of Lazarus being brought back to life—would be found in the written Word of God as a witness to all generations. It would demonstrate the scope of Jesus' authority, even over death. "Jesus said to her [Martha], 'I am the resurrection and the life. The one who believes in me will live, even though they die; and whoever lives by believing in me will never die. Do you believe this?'" (John 11:25-26).

What if they had known this outcome in their three-day waiting room? What if they could have somehow understood where this test was leading and how the story would end? But foreknowledge like that was not Jesus' plan for them, and neither is it for us. God allowed Mary and Martha to fret in the waiting room while He was working behind the scenes toward a greater purpose than they could have ever imagined. They already knew of Jesus' healing power, but they did not contemplate the what-if of a resurrection. And, too often, we don't contemplate the God-sized ending of our stories, either. We allow negative what-ifs to dominate and rarely consider any positive what-ifs. In my wildest dreams, I would not envision what God would do with Sam until years after my encounter at the bathroom mirror.

But God is "able to do immeasurably more than all we ask or imagine" (Ephesians 3:20). Do we believe that? I knew the verse and quoted it to others. But that it could really happen like that to me? I was doubtful, at best.

Even though transition is a difficult place to be, you were meant for this. One of the blessings of womanhood is waiting because that's when we get to see the astoundingly better ideas God has for us. While it may be a natural aspect of being a woman, it is not easy. You can be your own worst enemy by letting your mind play tricks on you. Or by doubting. Perhaps you don't really think your dream or hope will ever come to pass. Yet God is always up to something. He is not wasting any time or any of our experiences, for "we know that in all things God works for the good of those who love him, who have been called according to his purpose" (Romans 8:28). Our stories and journeys are waiting until Jesus' voice speaks, "Lazarus, come out" (John 11:43) and the dead situations—and the sleeping husbands—come to life.

We are called to faith that God may delay, but He is never late!

PRAY TOGETHER

Out of the depths I cry to you, LORD; Lord, hear my voice. Let your ears be attentive to my cry for mercy. If you, LORD, kept a record sins, Lord, who could stand? But with you there is forgiveness so that we can, with reverence, serve you. I wait for the LORD, my whole being waits, and in his word I put my hope. I wait for the Lord more than watchmen wait for the morning, more than watchmen wait for the morning.

—PSALM 130:1–6

Father, our hearts resonate with the cry of the psalmist! We cry to You from the depths. We know that You care for us and that You hear our voices. When we realize who You are, God, as compared to who we are, we can only cry for mercy. We cannot claim our own worthiness or merit. In fact, if You were to keep a record of our sins, we would not be able to stand before You. But with You there is forgiveness—and we humbly thank You. Because we are one flesh in our marriage, our unified souls wait for You, Lord. We put our hope only in You. Our souls wait for the Lord more than watchmen wait for the morning, more than watchmen wait for the morning! Amen.

SAY NO MORE
(THAN THE WORD)

*Your message on marital prayer has changed my family!
Immediately after arriving from the conference, I talked
with my wife about praying together through the Word.
My wife told me that she had been wanting this time, so it
is the real answer from God. The same day, we started to
pray through the Word of God from the Book of James. We
have already finished James, and now we are in the Book
of Ephesians.*

—PAUL

*My wife and I started praying together last Friday night
and have done it each night since. . . . Wonderful experience so far. We are also using the time to pray for our son.
I had been hitting the "snooze button" over the past few
months regarding praying for our young son—I think, in
part, because I couldn't get my arms around all that there
was to pray about. I was having trouble figuring out a
place to start. I now believe that praying the Bible was the
perfect way to start.*

—DUSTY

Near our home in Dallas, Texas, a 66-acre garden graces the southeastern shore of White Rock Lake. The Dallas Arboretum and Botanical Garden are nationally acclaimed and ranked by *USA Today* as one of the top attractions in the Dallas area. The southern climate, while blistering hot in summer, affords year round access to a stunning variety of flowers. Something is always in breathtaking bloom. Visitors stroll a network of winding paths to absorb the beauty of gardens and flowing fountains. Amid the vast array of plants and flowers, there are apparently 2,400 varieties of azaleas alone!

We explore the gardens periodically. And while enjoying the fragrances and visual beauty, we cannot help but ask ourselves, "How in the world do *they* maintain all these lawns, gardens, and flowers?" The amount of work and number of people it requires is staggering! If arboretum maintenance was neglected for even a short time, surely the grass would wither, and the flowers would fall.

The Apostle Peter draws on a similar image to emphasize several important contrasts in our lives. In 1 Peter 1:23-25, he points out:

> For you have been born again, not of perishable seed, but of imperishable, through the living and enduring word of God. For, "All men are like grass, and all their glory is like the flowers of the field; the grass withers and the flowers fall, but the word of the Lord endures forever."

Compared to the things of God, mankind and all the great things we accomplish are like fragile, vulnerable grass and flowers. People are frequently awed by their own accomplishments, but, the truth is, only the Word of the Lord stands forever.

The Word provides imperishable seed that gives birth to our spiritual lives, and only that kind of life endures forever. Our physical lives are perishable, even in their greatest, healthiest glory. Our spiritual lives, however, are initiated as well as nurtured with the eternal Word of the Lord.

The Word brings us life as we are born into the family of God and given a place in His kingdom. It's the perfect "garden maintenance" plan. The more we are seeded with the imperishable Word, the more we flower in spiritual life. We are guaranteed beauty, fruitfulness, and growth rather than temporary things that are certain to dry up and die.

As we commit ourselves to praying with the Word of the Lord as our guide, our hearts and minds are touched deeply with the imperishable seed Peter describes. This living and enduring Word stands forever in our prayers, bringing a transforming blessing, not only for our individual lives but for the life of our marriages.

EXPOSITORY PRAYING

You have likely heard of expository preaching and probably even experienced it in church. An expository preacher preaches through the Bible, verse by verse, paragraph by paragraph, allowing God's Word to deliver the message God's people need. The Bible guides preacher and congregation alike through the content, ideas, concepts, and exhortations God desires.

With the concept of expository preaching as a backdrop, you can begin to understand why we like to call our approach of praying Scripture "expository praying." As we follow the Bible with our prayers, God's Word guides us to the topics, ideas, praises, promises, blessings, confessions, and requests we most need to bring before Him. We "call out" God's Word in our prayers, and the Bible gives us the tracks to follow. This way, we can be sure our prayers are rich with imperishable seed.

PICK A BOOK OF THE BIBLE

Just as personal Bible study is more effective when you read consistently through Scripture rather than random verses here and there, praying through the Bible works better if you pray through books of the Bible together. That may sound daunting at first because you have never done anything like it before. We had been believers for multiple decades and married for as many, and we had never prayed through a book of the Bible before either. (In fact, we'd never even *heard* of doing such a thing.) This approach, however, has really energized us.

Even deciding together as husband and wife which book to start with can give you a sense of unity. Do either of you have a favorite book? If so, start there. Need a suggestion? We often recommend Philippians as a good starting point because it's a short book packed with great prayer material. Another good starting place is the Psalms. Since it is a book of songs (essentially prayers with rhythm and tune), the words of the Psalms provide a perfect guide for praying. You can voice your prayers in the very same words David brought before the Lord.

Praying through books of the Bible keeps you on the path. It gives a plan to follow, and it is easy to remember where you left off. Having a plan seems to be especially helpful for husbands to know where you're going together. The book you pray through becomes a map or a blueprint to guide you.

Wherever you decide to begin, you'll be amazed at how the Holy Spirit will make His presence evident, from time to time, in very clear ways. This happens, of course, because He is faithful to His Word but also because, as we pray through books of the Bible, we are actually learning together at the same time. Although the immediate purpose is not to study the Bible, our minds grow and are transformed (Romans 12:2) from exposure to God's truth as our hearts reach out to God together in prayer.

To jump-start your prayer together, the appendix of this book provides a guide for praying through the Book of James. We've divided the Epistle of James into sections and suggest a sample prayer that follows the flow and content from the verses. Try praying through James together, and once you've done it, we are confident the Holy Spirit will encourage you to keep going with other books!

THREE STEPS FOR PRAYING THE WORD TOGETHER

1. Read.

Read a reasonable number of Bible verses out loud. Don't try to bite off too much. Choosing how many verses to cover is a judgment call you make each time. Just remember: this is not a Bible Study, it is a time of prayer. The husband is not coming to teach the Bible to his wife, nor is the wife teaching the Bible to her husband. Together, you are coming before the Lord and asking Him to reveal content and topics to pray about.

Read your verses slowly, and let the meaning sink in. Both of you can participate in reading the selection, of course. And this may go without saying, but it is important to read from the same version of the Bible.

2. Observe.

Once we've read the passage, we usually sit quietly for a minute or two to think about what we have just read. That gives the Holy Spirit a chance to speak to our hearts, so He can help us make a few observations from the verses. What jumps out from the reading? Are there any key words, phrases, or concepts that stand out? What is the main idea or topic in these verses? What was the author saying to the readers of his day? Which of those truths are also meaningful to us today? Does the reading prompt any special thoughts or insights? Does an immediate application come to mind? You can answer as many or as few of these questions as you feel led to. The idea is simply to pay attention to what God wants to speak to you from this particular Scripture.

A good way to think about this step is that we are looking for "prayer points" such as a:

* Promise to realize
* Praise to lift to God for His character or activity
* Sin to confess
* Command to obey
* Warning to heed
* Path to pursue
* Fact to remember
* Truth to be renewed in our hearts
* Doctrine to understand
* Encouragement to receive
* Thanksgiving to lift up
* Anything else the Holy Spirit shows us from the Word

Following this process, you can take turns sharing with one another what you see in the Scriptures. You are on "holy ground" as you come together in the one-flesh spiritual intimacy of your marriage. The Holy Spirit will meet you to encourage, direct, rebuke, love, bring joy, offer peace, remind you of truth, and more. The beauty of doing this is that you are before the Lord in unity. This sort of prayer weaves together the strands of your marriage, your prayers, and the Word of God into one strong cord. You will hear your husband's or wife's heart more intimately as you listen to how the Lord speaks to him or her from His Word.

3. Pray.

Take turns praying out loud for a short time. Follow what the Holy Spirit shows as the focus for the content and flow of your prayers. Pray these things for one another, over your marriage, over your children, and however else you feel led. In doing so, you will be praying the flow of what the Lord has written. Sometimes when we pray, our prayers consist of words directly from the verses. We simply turn the verses into prayers and pray God's Word back to Him.

Another helpful approach is to personalize the verses in your prayers by calling out the names of people who come to your heart and mind. In this way, you are covering your beloved family and friends with prayers that reflect the very heart of God.

Also, be sure to bring into your prayers the issues facing you each day. You can present to the Lord the concerns of your hearts. What is happening today that might worry you? What warrants thanksgiving and praise to the Lord? Tell God the "now" issues that surround you. Even though God already knows everything, as you pray your concerns, they flow through your heart in a way that can bring better perspective, deeper peace, and more genuine praises which you might not have otherwise experienced.

And, finally, this may seem obvious, but remember that you are talking to the living God in your prayers, not to one another. God is the audience. He is turning His ear to the unified voice of your marriage.

FRESHNESS AND VITALITY

Both of us came from religious backgrounds that taught and modeled for us that our prayers consisted of reciting memorized words, which have been passed down through the centuries. We both vividly recall reciting such prayers mindlessly on many occasions. Yet that is all we knew to do. This is not to say there is anything wrong with the great creeds and prayers of church history, but many people slip into the trap of simply reciting memorized prayers. Then they wonder why they lack a vital connection with God in prayer.

In the providence of God, we trusted in Jesus Christ as our Savior during our college days. In fact, while we were dating, the Lord brought each of us to Himself during the same week through completely different encounters with friends. Vicki came to the Lord at a Bible study a friend invited her to on a Tuesday evening. Then that Friday evening, Sam visited a friend in the hospital who was dying of cancer. While there, a pastor also happened to be visiting, and he shared the gospel with Sam. We thank God for this amazing blessing and wonderful timing.

The two of us attended Bible studies when we were new believers, and we remember being fascinated by the prayers of the group leader. When it came time to pray, he launched into a spontaneous, out-loud conversation with God, and he always seemed know exactly what to say.

What's more, it quickly became evident that other people in the group *also* knew how to fashion words to their prayers. People took turns, one by one, talking out loud to God. They were creative and offered splendid, heartfelt prayers right off the top of their heads! We still amuse ourselves at thinking back on how panicked we sometimes felt. Hearts pounding, we worried, "Oh no, what if they expect us to do this, too?" But thankfully—and to the credit of group leaders and their sensitivity to folks like us—that didn't happen.

In time, though, we recognized that, as Christians, we needed to somehow learn to pray like this. We thought we needed to be ready, on the spot, at any time, to launch into an extemporaneous (and as eloquent as possible) prayer to God. We thought we had to impress everyone in the group, and remember that God just might be listening, too. Phew! A lot of pressure!

Perhaps these words and emotions from our past reflect how one or both of you feel when you think about praying with each other. It is not uncommon to hesitate about praying out loud. Some people regard prayer as a deeply personal thing, and they are reluctant to pray with someone else, but in truth, that is all the more reason we suggest that the Bible is the perfect guide to finding the words to pray. Many times, we have seen this model for prayers in marriage become a connecting point for a couple's growth.

Some Christians, of course, are completely comfortable voicing spontaneous prayers. In fact, they might be very experienced and "good at it." Perhaps you are already used to praying out loud and have been doing it for years. Even so, we would suggest that following the Bible to provide the content and focus of your prayers will bring freshness and vitality. Whether praying out loud comes naturally to you or not, we've provided below a few samples of how praying Scripture can work for you.

EXAMPLES OF SCRIPTURE PRAYERS

Grace and peace to you from God our Father and the Lord
Jesus Christ, who gave himself for our sins to rescue us

from the present evil age, according to the will of our God
and Father, to whom be glory forever and ever. Amen.

—GALATIANS 1:3–5

Husband's Prayer

"Father, we are reminded from Your Word today that You are a God of grace and peace. We thank You that grace and peace are coming to our marriage and family today from God who is our Father, through our relationship with Jesus Christ. We are deeply blessed to know that Jesus gave Himself on the Cross to die for our sins to rescue us from the present evil age. The salvation You have given us is from Your grace. This salvation and the relationship we have with You give us peace. We are humbled for these blessings, Lord. Amen."

Wife's Prayer

"Lord, we give praise to You this day because these provisions of grace, peace, and salvation have been given to us according to Your will for our lives. We ask that Your grace and peace would come over our children as they move through their lives today. In this world, we confess that every day our family is subjected to and can be vulnerable to the evil that is so present. So we pray that Your grace and peace would protect and comfort us. We agree with what the Bible says— that all glory is due to You, God, forever and ever. Amen."

My dear brothers and sisters, take note of this: Everyone
should be quick to listen, slow to speak and slow to become
angry, because human anger does not produce the righ-
teousness that God desires. Therefore get rid of all moral

filth and the evil that is so prevalent and humbly accept the word planted in you, which can save you.

—JAMES 1:19–21

Husband's Prayer

"Father in heaven, the Bible is very practical and meaningful to us. Especially today, we ask You to help us be quick to listen—quick to listen to You, quick to listen to one another, and quick to listen to the people around us, within our family and wherever we go. Lord, we also know that when we become angry that man's anger does not bring about the righteous life that You desire for us. Therefore, I pray over our family a better sense of listening, and that You would calm the anger that can arise in our hearts. Amen."

Wife's Prayer

"Lord, we also see in the Book of James today that we need to be slow to speak. We confess to You that sometimes we speak out before we really hear. Sometimes when people are speaking, we are not listening but instead are already preparing what we want to say. Lord, give us ears to hear better today! We also confess that there is moral filth and evil in the world, especially facing our children and teenagers. We have sought to plant the Word in their lives over the years. So today, Lord, we pray that You would work in their hearts in such a way that they would humbly accept Your Word and be quick to listen to Your Holy Spirit. Amen."

In the past God spoke to our ancestors through the prophets at many times and in various ways, but in these last

days he has spoken to us by his Son, whom he appointed heir of all things, and through whom also he made the universe. The Son is the radiance of God's glory and the exact representation of his being, sustaining all things by his powerful word. After he had provided purification for sins, he sat down at the right hand of the Majesty in heaven.

—HEBREWS 1:1–3

Husband's Prayer

"Father, we thank You that in the past You have spoken to us through the prophets in many ways. But, Lord, we thank You that we live in the last days, during which You have spoken to us through Your Son, Jesus Christ! We thank You that Jesus has been appointed heir of all things. We thank You that You have created the universe through Jesus. Amen."

Wife's Prayer

"The Son is the radiance of God's glory and the exact representation of His being. We thank You that Jesus sustains all things by His powerful Word. We praise You that Jesus has provided purification for our sins and that He is now seated at the right hand of the Majesty in heaven. And we thank You that Jesus is superior to any and all of the angels and that He has inherited a name that is superior to the name of any angel! Amen."

Praying like this over time will bring increasing richness, energy, strength, and a sense of connectedness to our prayers. As Dietrich Bonhoeffer once said, "The richness of God's word ought to determine our prayer, not the poverty of our heart."

SOME PRACTICAL CONSIDERATIONS

Life gets pretty big sometimes, so it's understandable if you wonder how to work in this time of praying together as husband and wife. We've asked ourselves (many times!) the questions outlined below and offer to you the answers we've found to be the most helpful.

1. When are we going to do this?

Determine what works for your marriage considering the context of your family. For some couples, early morning prayer together is good. For others, praying in the evening or just before bedtime is best. The ages and stages of the children living under your roof will surely influence the time of day that will work. You may have to manage young children morning, noon, and night. Or perhaps you have teen-agers running in and out of the house at all hours. And maybe both! In some marriages, the husband is delighted to rise before the sun, but the wife is the proverbial night owl—or the other way around.

Obviously, there is no perfect time of the day that can be applied consistently by all of us. The core answer to the "when" question is that you believe in the importance of marital prayer so much that you are resolved to make the sacrifices and compromises required for you to make the time to pray together. And if *our* experience is any indicator, be forewarned that, as soon as you feel like you've achieved the ideal rhythm for praying together, *something* will arise to send you back to the drawing board.

What could possibly get in the way and disrupt a commitment to prayer in marriage? How about:

❖ The pace of life in most families

❖ The changing seasons across spring, summer, fall, and winter

✤ Business travel

✤ Vacation times

✤ The ups and downs of tension

✤ Disagreements and differing perspectives

✤ Dynamic schedules for each and every family member

I'm sure we could go on.

These modern-day realities—and our own experience on this journey—are why we suggest that you start small and work your way up to more consistent times together. We do *not* recommend that you plan on praying together every single day. To do that would throw a wrench in the works from the very beginning. It's just not realistic for most couples. So, with that reality in focus, we are simply encouraging you to go for marital prayer that is more intentional and more regular than you've ever done before—agreeing in advance that daily prayer is not even a reasonable goal. It will give you a greater sense of freedom to pray and increase your chances for success in praying together regularly.

2. How much time should it take?

Recognizing the real life demands and struggles we just mentioned, we recommend you plan for a short prayertime. Quantity of time does not necessarily translate into quality of spiritual growth and oneness. Since praying a particular book of the Bible is your path, simply pick up where you left off from the previous prayertime each time you pray. Follow the routine: read the next several verses, determine prayer points, and pray together, focusing on what the Holy Spirit has revealed. Ten minutes, 15 minutes, 20? See how the Spirit leads you.

You'll also want to be open to the possibility that there will be some occasions when you are not in a hurry. As the Holy Spirit leads, and discussion flows between the two of you, the time can pass quickly. Enjoy special times like these!

Although you might not be able to imagine ever spending an hour or more in prayer and spiritual discussion together, there may come wonderful, extended seasons of prayer in your marriage as you walk this way together. Why? Because you will be following a determined path of praying what God is showing through His Word.

3. What if we miss?

In this journey of praying together, there is one thing that we can absolutely, positively guarantee you: sometimes you will skip, postpone, or otherwise miss your planned prayertimes together. Life can be crazy. Our fast pace pushes us, like Superman, "faster than a speeding bullet." Yet we are not supermen and superwomen. That's one reason we suggest that you do not need to make *daily* prayer together the goal. You may even have to miss your prayertimes fairly regularly—certainly more often than you really want to. But trust us, that's OK. You may even miss several days in a row for one reason or the other, but do not let that discourage you!

Over the years we've tried different models, methods, or approaches to finding time to connect spiritually, but no plan lasts indefinitely. What we can tell you is that praying through books of the Bible has a sort of spiritual and practical "stickiness" to it. Your praying-the-Bible track will make it easier to get back on track when you miss time(s) together. When we agreed to pray through the Word of God, it meant that all we had to do was return to the place in the Bible where we prayed last time and keep going. Like the tortoise and the hare, slow and steady wins the race! The Bible will keep you on track. You just need to add the "slow and steady."

4. How long should we continue doing this?

What if you were to match the length of commitment you pledged to one another on your wedding day? *Until death do us part.*

In our marriages, we are one flesh for all of our lives on this side of eternity. Intentional spiritual intimacy around the living Word of God as husband and wife is an anointed expression of oneness in God for a lifetime.

As long as we are breathing, disciples of Jesus Christ are called to pursue growth and maturity. No one ever finishes that race. There is no such thing as a fully completed follower of Jesus.

As much as this is true for individual believers, so it is true of every marriage that claims the name of Jesus. While there are many dimensions of growing together in a Christian marriage, praying through the Word of God can become a core component of your relationship. If you start praying the Word together in your marriage, what good reason would ever cause you to stop? Most likely, nothing until death do you part!

The timing of God's work in our lives is always amazing. Sometimes, we go to church and hear a message preached from the Bible that is exactly what we needed to hear that day. When that happens, God is speaking to us through the one ministering the Word of God. Similarly, in our prayer journey through God's Word, the Holy Spirit will providentially bring to you exactly what is relevant for you to pray about. You will experience God's voice together through His Word—not in some sort of strange, mystical encounter, but in the reality of connecting with one another, with God, and His Word.

PRAY TOGETHER

For you have been born again, not of perishable seed, but of imperishable, through the living and enduring word of God. For, "All people are like grass, and all their glory is like the flowers of the field; the grass withers and the flowers fall, but the word of the Lord endures forever." And this is the word that was preached to you.

—1 PETER 1:23–25

Father, we have been born again, not of perishable seed, but of the imperishable seed, through the living and enduring Word of God. As all people, we are like grass, and our glory is like the flowers of the fields, which eventually falls, or as the grass that eventually withers. As we learn to let the Bible become a guide to inform our prayers together, we are confident You are giving us enduring and eternal words and truths. Your Word has been a source to feed our souls through preaching, but now, also feed our souls through praying! Thank You, Lord, for Your enduring Word. Amen.

CHAPTER 6

INTENTIONAL SPIRITUAL INTIMACY

It seems that lots of us husbands share a common issue: we struggle to spiritually lead our wives, especially in an intentional way. Ironically, it seems that lots of wives share a common desire: for husbands to rise to the occasion and lead more in the home.

—PASTOR ARTHUR

I have been struggling with this issue for many years. And as I have explained to many of my family and friends since attending your session at our church men's breakfast, I've had the "directional compass" in my back pocket for years . . . but what I was missing is the "specific map." You gave me the map and I am very excited about that. I can see what a powerful message this is, and I would like the opportunity to help further it. I've personally been searching for this for years, and I can see where there must be many, many men out there that are doing the same thing . . . and for the most part, we don't even know we are searching for it.

—BOBBIE

Marriage has been appropriately illustrated as a triangle. God is at the top of the triangle. Husband and wife are at each of the bottom corners. As husband and wife draw near to God, moving up their respective sides of the triangle, they move closer to one another at the same time. The triangle illustrates the benefit of having God as the focus of your marriage relationship.

THREE'S *GREAT* COMPANY

Orthodox Christian faith embraces the mysterious reality revealed in the Bible that God exists as a Trinity: Father, Son, and Holy Spirit. Three persons are one God. Christian marriage may be understood as a reflection, however imperfect, of the holy Trinity. Three persons constitute one Christian marriage: God, husband, and wife. Christian reality defies normal mathematics because one plus one plus one equals *one!* Oneness, harmony, unity, togetherness, and solidarity represent the primary intention of marriage—not only with one another as husband and wife but as husband and wife with God!

Praying the Word of God *together* helps this dynamic trio spring to life. A husband/wife/God prayer journey is the triangle lived out in a practical and real manner. God does not want to be left behind at the marriage altar. He wants to go with us on our journey of life.

Imagine this marriage triangle as an electrical circuit. A complete circuit is required for the power to flow, and a short circuit happens when the wires are not properly connected. If we experience a short circuit, we wiggle the wires and generate intermittent surges of power. This is like our marriages when we bumble along, haphazardly connecting spiritually.

Praying together completes the marriage triangle circuit. Connecting in your one-flesh spiritual union by praying the Bible together activates the power, presence, and perspectives of God over our marriages, lives, children, families, ministries, and careers. This is not a gimmick for manipulating God to do what we want Him to do. It is a call to enter deeper into God's sacred design for the union of marriage, and it's a doable way to make it happen. We can connect more intentionally as we use the Bible to guide our prayers together.

BACK TO GENESIS

Look at God's description of marriage in Genesis 2:24-25 using the words *one flesh*: "That is why a man leaves his father and mother and is united to his wife, and they become one flesh. Adam and his wife were both naked, and they felt no shame."

An in-depth look at this passage is beyond our scope and purpose, but we need to recognize God's basic description of marriage. The key ideas are not difficult to identify:

✤ Leave
✤ Cleave
✤ One flesh
✤ Naked and not ashamed

The man is to leave his family of origin, to join together with his wife as "one flesh." The relationship is intimate in every dimension. There is no shame.

Husband and wife are "one flesh" before God. This is not simply a metaphor, idea, or illustration. This is a spiritual, mystical reality before God. Yes, God sees the Christian husband and wife, each as an individual child before Him, but in the union of marriage, they are *one*. So normal mathematics is defied again: one plus one—equals *one*. This is a critical reality to grasp. We know it, but do we really understand it?

UNION = LIFE

God designed our bodies so that when a husband and wife come together in sexual intimacy, life is created. Our joining each other has life-creating, life-giving power. Physical union yields physical life.

As a result of physical intimacy, children are conceived and birthed. From the physical union between us, God chose to create three daughters who are eternal beings. When you pause to think about it, that is astounding! In this one-flesh connection, God ordained creative power. He told Adam and Eve to go forth, multiply, and "fill the earth" (Genesis 1:28). This one-flesh idea is one command from God men are always delighted to obey: "Oh, yes, God. Whatever you say, Lord!"

What we often overlook is that the same life-generating dynamic happens with spiritual intimacy as well. *Spiritual union yields enhanced vitality and growth in our spiritual life together.* When we come together spiritually, in prayer, God conceives and births life—His life—through our spiritual oneness. He can bring to life:

❖ Insights

❖ Ideas

❖ Love

❖ Joy

❖ Peace

❖ Answered Prayers

❖ Emotional Health

❖ Transparency and Honesty

❖ Spiritual Growth

❖ Unity

Spiritual connection also brings with it a unique emotional connection, and the combination of the two can be very powerful. In fact, this may be difficult for us to imagine, but our prayers as husband and wife can have the chemistry of creating more spiritual and emotional vitality and life among us than the prayers we would pray with anyone else. Because of our one-flesh union, and our cooperation with God, praying together in marriage is more important than the prayers in which we engage with any other person.

GOOD COVERAGE

Imagine a spiritual umbrella covering your marriage, family, life, and ministry. The life-giving power of God spreads over everything. By praying the Word of God, the will of God, His values, truths, principles, and blessings, the Spirit's intercessions from the Bible pour vitality into our lives and over our children. What an exciting opportunity! At a minimum, think of how important is it to pray the Word over the children and grandchildren God has given to you.

Wives need this connection. Husbands need this connection. Our children need this connection. Our grandchildren need this connection. The spiritual union of your marriage covers your lives and your whole family. What a formidable spiritual reality!

EASY AND BEARING FRUIT

Two illustrations from the teachings of Jesus center on the important concept of connectedness: the yoke and the vine. In Matthew 11:28-30, Jesus calls us to take on His yoke so we can learn from Him:

Come to me, all you who are weary and burdened, and I will give you rest. Take my yoke upon you and learn from me, for I am gentle and humble in heart, and you will find rest for your souls. For my yoke is easy and my burden is light.

And in John 15:4-5, Jesus reveals the necessity of the branch remaining in connection with the vine to yield fruit:

Remain in me, as I also remain in you. No branch can bear fruit by itself; it must remain in the vine. Neither can you bear fruit unless you remain in me. I am the vine; you are the branches. If you remain in me and I in you, you will bear much fruit; apart from me you can do nothing.

With these two illustrations, Jesus calls us to connect with God. This is the only path to rest and fruitfulness. As we pointed out earlier, God exists as a Trinity, and His perfect desire for union and connectedness is reflected in the creation of marriage as a one-flesh relationship. Praying as one is a practical way to learn together from the gentle, humble heart of Jesus Christ and become increasingly fruitful for our joy and His glory.

LIVING WITH DEPRIVATION

A healthy marriage will include a diet of mutually satisfying physical intimacy. We realize sticking to this diet is complex, and every marriage needs to work toward what is acceptable for both partners. In Genesis 2:24–25 NASB, the climactic result of the one-flesh marriage union is naked and not ashamed. Yes, this verse refers to the physical nakedness of husband and wife before one another, but that is not all. God's intent is that, in the unique relationship of marriage, there is openness and vulnerability—without shame—in every dimension. This is the safety, security, and acceptance the human heart longs for. It is the intimacy that allows for understanding and growth together.

We are not attempting to address the complexity of issues surrounding sexual intimacy in marriage here. Our point is that holistic marital health requires emotional, physical, *and* spiritual well-being. The three are interrelated. Typically, men more regularly desire and need sexual intimacy. Men know it. Their wives know it. But how important is attention to spiritual and emotional needs? Sometimes men expect wives to be available physically, but husbands might not be so available to their wives emotionally and spiritually. Perhaps husbands have taught their wives to learn to live with deprivation. If so, husbands need to face a hard question. How would we fare, if our wives were not available for our physical needs? Yet have we abdicated our responsibility, depriving her of spiritual and emotional intimacy?

Sometimes husbands think they are disqualified from spiritual intimacy with their wives because of the "issues," sins, and shortcomings in their own lives. But we dare say they rarely, if ever, disqualify themselves from physical intimacy because of those same concerns! When is the last time a husband said, "Honey, let's not have sex because I have some struggles in my life"? It seems husbands are good at compartmentalizing things when it comes to sexual intimacy, but what is that about?

During part of the wake-up conversation in our living room that afternoon, Vicki actually said to Sam, "Honey, if we had sexual intimacy as often as we prayed together, you would be pretty disappointed." Wow, that's not pulling any punches! You are welcome to laugh, but how true is it in your marriage?

The bottom line is this: *if we are making time in our marriage for physical intimacy, we need to be making time for spiritual intimacy.* Tension over physical intimacy in marriage is a common issue, and neither of us is minimizing this complicated reality at all. If we were to connect more consistently spiritually and emotionally, though, the benefits and blessings are likely to show up in physical intimacy as well.

Think of it in this way:

✤ Physical one-flesh intimacy creates physical life.
✤ Spiritual one-flesh intimacy enhances spiritual vitality and growth.

When a husband and wife come together in the physical union of marriage, in the providence of God, children are conceived and birthed. No physical intimacy, no new physical life comes forth. We need to realize spiritual intimacy in a parallel fashion. In order for spiritual life to be conceived, birthed, and live in our marriages, we must come together in spiritual intention and intimacy. Clearly, praying together with the Scriptures is not the only way, but we strongly suggest it is a core way to enhance holistic intimacy—"naked and not ashamed"—in many dimensions of life and marriage.

INTENTIONALISM, NOT LEGALISM

Some people are afraid to follow patterns in their Christian walk because they think that means they're being legalistic, but when it comes to praying the Scriptures, that simply is not the case. The pattern is "new every morning" (Lamentations 3:23), and the plan is simple: husbands become more intentional (less haphazard) in spiritual leadership. Using the Bible as a prayer guide, both husband and wife are equipped with an approach that is comfortable and helpful to take on the yoke and tap into the Vine.

And exactly why isn't this a form of legalism? Legalism can be described as seeking the approval and favor of God through following rules or engaging in a certain set of behaviors. And sometimes such behaviors are meant simply to impress other people.

Neither of these dysfunctional reasons to pray is part of what we suggest. Praying the Scriptures is not a slavish rule for your marriage but rather a healthy and holy routine (and one that can flex with the requirements of your schedule), offering real connectedness in your marriage. Through it, you have the opportunity to enter into the originally intended design and flow of marriage as three come into union: God, husband, and wife.

PRAY TOGETHER

"For this reason a man will leave his father and mother and be united to his wife, and the two will become one flesh." This is a profound mystery—but I am talking about Christ and the church. However, each one of you also must love his wife as he loves himself, and the wife must respect her husband.

—EPHESIANS 5:31–33

God, we pray today for unity in our marriage as reflected by this important phrase: one flesh. We acknowledge that our marriage represents the relationship between Jesus Christ and His bride, the church. That truth is humbling and convicting to us, Lord. We see two fundamental fuels for our marriage: love and respect. A husband is to love his wife as he loves himself! And the wife is clearly called to respect her husband. Father, empower our marriage with fresh love and genuine respect, so this profound mystery may bring glory to You, security to our family, and joy to our marriage. Amen. ⌁

CHAPTER 7

INTIMACY AND THE HURTS OF A WOMAN'S HEART

(BY VICKI)

My husband and I have been praying through the Word, and it's been so amazing.

—CRYSTAL

We have been enjoying working our way through Philippians without stressing about "doing a study." Thanks!

—TABITHA

My wife and I have started our prayertimes together, and we're excited about it. She had me explain to our youngest daughter and her new husband what we're doing. . . hoping to influence them to join us. We're starting with Philippians, and the first day we got to, "I thank God upon every remembrance of you," and we thanked God for a plethora of people in our lives. My wife started thanking the Lord for those who have hurt us in ministry (thankfully, not too many) . . . thanking God for them and how He used them for our good. She was crying . . . it was a wonderful experience for the two of us. And that was just the first day! We're on the journey with you.

—RICK

S am enrolled in summer seminary classes when I was a young
mother trying to manage two children under the age of five. We
moved into a small apartment close to the seminary, planning to live
there for three months. Little did I know how tight the quarters
would feel to our family of four.

We attended a nearby church, and one Sunday morning as we
started the drive back home, Sam flipped on the radio. "Every Day
with Jesus," a popular song at the time, bubbled happily out of the
speakers. But other things bubbled inside of me. My overwhelmed
heart screamed silently, and I slapped the "off" button on the radio.
I answered Sam's "what-just-happened?" look with silence. Inwardly,
though, I shouted at God: *That is not true for me! These people are
either lying or delusional, or they have something I'm not experiencing!
So, if this is real—if You are real—I need You to help me figure this out!*
There was no "dear Jesus" at the beginning or "in Jesus' name" at
the end—just a heart-wrenching, soul cry from feeling overwhelmed,
emotionally upended, and totally helpless to address the misery I was
feeling.

At the time, I had no idea what was happening in me or how it
was affecting my prayer life or, for that matter, any type of intimacy
with God—or my spiritual relationship with Sam. Now, 35 years after
that stressed-out day, I have a pretty good understanding of my problem. I had a lot going on deep inside that needed to be addressed.
I had some serious unpacking to do!

ALL PACKED, BUT NOWHERE
NEAR READY TO GO

When couples come to the marriage altar, they are prepared to
exchange vows, celebrate with friends and family, and above all,

spend time with a new spouse on what they assume will be a dreamy honeymoon. We pack our suitcases for that special trip, but what we don't realize is everything else we're taking with us—for these special days and every other day of our married lives.

We arrive at the altar with invisible emotional suitcases packed with expectations, fears, perspectives, attitudes, and beliefs we've been collecting since the day we were born. Some are healthy and some are *not!* This unseen luggage affects every aspect of our married lives—including the spiritual intimacy and prayer life we share with our husbands. On our wedding day, I had no idea that my suitcase even existed. Over the years, though, my awareness of it and the unpacking of its contents has been critical to preparing me for spiritual oneness with Sam and our enhanced prayer life together.

Early on, I had no concept of how past events and subsequent unresolved emotions affected me and how they would impact my future. They were a powerful force, dominating my behavior, and I didn't even know they were there.

Sam and I attended premarital counseling, and the sessions addressed some common challenges of our future life together. It helped, but not as much as I supposed it had. I thought the past was the past, and as long as I could remember, my parents taught me that whatever the problems or disappointments you face, you just move on.

To my surprise, as life with Sam began, I discovered that situations repeatedly seemed to *not* bring out the best in me. In fact, some situations absolutely brought out the very worst. Attitudes, reactions, feelings, fear, anxiety, and just plain unhappiness flooded out. The happily-ever-after promise I believed would occur simply was not what I experienced. Instead I experienced: depression, anger, and extreme disappointment with life because I was not getting what I expected. Of course, the only thing I could see in my life that had changed was that I had gotten married. So my simple logic provided the only possible conclusion: *my husband is causing all this*. Certainly, he—as all men—brought his own invisible suitcase into our marriage, but the lesson for me was that God wanted to unpack *my* emotional suitcase by *using* my marriage as a tool for the job. That certainly wasn't what I thought I had signed up for.

Before saying our wedding vows, all of us accumulate a lifetime-to-that-point of good, bad, and ugly emotions and events. Most of us, though, have either been ill-equipped to process the emotions that came with the events, were too young and inexperienced to be aware of the emotions, or were not allowed to express what we were feeling. From my family of origin, I learned to stuff my emotions as I went along. The pace of life and the demands of raising five children did not afford my parents much time for anything but work, eat, and sleep. That is just the way it was growing up in the 1950s and '60s.

While I do not begrudge my upbringing, I do recognize that it left me poorly prepared to handle my emotions in a healthy way. I simply adopted my parents' approach of living with unprocessed emotions. It may have helped me survive my early years of hurt and confusion, but in the long run, those emotions began to resurface and do some real damage.

So as I reflect now on what I brought into my marriage, I think if Sam could have seen all of it at one glance, the ceremony might have ended abruptly: "I don't" rather than "I do." And I suspect many other marriage ceremonies might have the same conclusion!

TWO TYPES OF SUITCASES

From observations in my 40-year marriage and from observing human nature during 35 years in Christian ministry, I've come to think that we all carry two types of suitcases: *universal* baggage and *individual* baggage. We all struggle with anger, bitterness, jealousy, and pride. This is the universal baggage that comes with our innately sinful selves. Everyone has these sin problems. Where things get tricky, though, is when our individual baggage gets in the way.

While our lives may be similar with respect to sin, the effect of our individual issues on our inner suitcases can differ greatly. These issues have been shaped by life's events, usually trauma and a lack of processing trauma with the truth. If we don't process truthfully, we will never be prepared for the type of emotional and spiritual intimacy God desires us to have with our spouses. God used Sam to uncover one of my issues, a lie I had believed from childhood, which greatly undermined our intimacy as well as my emotional stability.

Sam was serving on the pastoral staff of our church at the time and because of his giftedness as a teacher, he was occasionally asked to lead a women's Bible study. As he left the house to teach the women's group one day, a cloud of rejection settled over me. I felt as if Sam had been emotionally absent the last few days. *Other women's needs are more important than mine*, I thought. After talking to a counselor friend of mine, I realized my fear of rejection stemmed from a child-hood trauma. While my father had been physically present, he was always emotionally distant, leaving me feeling abandoned by him. That baggage multiplied my reaction to Sam. Once I discovered the real source of my problem, though, I put my present-day situation into perspective and dismantled this lie that separated me from Sam. My heart had been filled with what 2 Corinthians 10:5 (ASV) calls vain "imaginations, and every high thing that is exalted against the knowledge of God."

Scenarios like this have played out many times, but I have come to understand that it is not our traumas that define us; it is what we tell ourselves about the trauma. My father's emotional distance, for example, prompted me to adopt the belief that men are not really interested in relationships at an emotional level. So, early in my marriage, I projected that view of men onto Sam. I chose to believe that my needs must not be important, and so I would not even communicate them. Talk about putting Sam in a double bind!

THE UNIVERSITY OF ONE FLESH

Marriage is an incredibly powerful institution for helping us unpack our invisible suitcases. Like most brides, I stood at the altar, excited to embark on my new married life. I didn't realize, though, that my vows enrolled me in the University of One Flesh and an amazing opportunity to achieve freedom in knowing my spouse and myself. But the price would be to allow God to unpack my emotional mess!

God's course of instruction included using my husband as an object lesson. Through how I interacted with him, God would reveal what was really in me and would free me from the incorrect belief systems I had so systematically formed as I packed. God gradually inserted Himself and the truths of His Word into my mind and, little by little, better thinking changed my feelings. My behavior adjusted, too, and spiritual intimacy with Sam grew deeper.

PROCESS IT!

A supposed solution to handling emotional issues these days is "deal with it; get over it." But in a practical, day-to-day sense, how do we do this? Is there a formula? A pill to take? Is there a Bible verse to claim so a spiritual magic wand zaps the issue out of existence? Does time cause our crammed emotions to self-resolve and evaporate? Do we just grow out of our problems? If I read a book, attend a conference, talk to a friend, and hear the right sermon, will my inner hurt be resolved?

While any of these possibilities can be part of the solution, none of them is the silver bullet. By God's grace, I have experienced what we should really encourage each other to do in order to "deal with it" in a healthy way. The whole answer is to *process it*. Only as we process the lies we believed and the emotions associated with them, can we avoid the stuffing syndrome. If we *process as we go*, we can lead lives uncluttered by damaging emotions. Then, and only then, can we live in the *present* and carry light, empty suitcases!

I believe this is what God and the Scriptures refer to when talking about *sanctification*. Sanctification happens in our souls, and it is a . . . process. As we go through life, God continually replaces the lies we believed with the truth of His Word. Instead of falsehoods, we can embrace powerful truths about ourselves, God, and others—especially our husbands. *Truth* gives us the peace, joy, and freedom God wants us to have. Jesus said in John 8:32 (NKJV), "You shall know the truth, and the truth shall make you free." Typically, God uses external circumstances and relationships with husbands and children to expose the lies and false beliefs in which we are entangled. Each of us packed our bags in our family of origin, and now God uses our current family to help us unpack. It is divinely orchestrated and systematically arranged by our heavenly Father who loves us deeply and wants us to experience the abundant life He promised—from the inside out.

WHERE DID I STUFF MY STUFF?

Our inner suitcases are comprised of three overlapping compartments: mind, will, and emotions. If we have stuffed our emotions for years and not processed along the way, they may speak loudly, but unfortunately the source can be difficult to identify. When unprocessed emotions have been stuffed, our minds fill with the untruths we have believed, and our souls suffer. Our wills are then dictated by our minds, controlled by emotion. But God desires that our *minds* be renewed, so our *wills* can respond, and then our *emotions* can follow in wholeness and truth. This is the order God designed for the spiritual health that enhances relational intimacy and spiritual oneness with our husbands. God desires our cooperation, yet He will not violate our integrity as persons. He desires our willingness. He desires our submission.

So this brings us to a few crucial questions: Are you willing to get seriously honest with yourself and admit that you need to face and unpack your emotional suitcase? Are you tired of the same old swings of your heart? Are you exhausted from using human resources to manage your repressed emotions? Are you willing to do whatever it takes to allow God to lead in processing your baggage? Are you willing to move past blaming other people and playing the victim and take more personal responsibility than ever before?

Possibly it is *your* time to do some soul searching or, I should say, to allow God to do the soul searching. He is the only One who knows where to start. It can be overwhelming and, quite honestly, depressing to start unpacking. It can also be painful (I often refer to it as "heart surgery without anesthesia") but if you're going to grow in genuine spiritual intimacy with your husband, you have to process these unhealthy emotions. Your prayers will falter until you do.

My unpacking began the day I turned off the radio in disgust at the "Every Day with Jesus" song. I didn't realize it at the time, but I invited God to take over my stuffed suitcase. When I told God that He would have to help me figure out what I was feeling, He started helping me process all of the hidden stuff. I did not have a clue where to start, but He did. He just wanted my permission and my cooperation. He was waiting to help, waiting for me to come to the end of myself to reach out and include Him in the process. I had never seen either of my parents involve God or Jesus in their lives in this practical way. They had modeled only "grit your teeth and get through it." But that was not working for me! I wanted something more and hoped God could really pull this off. I had my doubts, but desperation overrode them.

A MESSY PACKER

Sam and I travel a lot on our overseas missions, but no matter how many trips we take, it is always a struggle for me to pack my suitcase efficiently. Sam, though, is a packing machine. He has it down to a science, and although I have learned a lot from him and his "packing checklist," for me, loading my suitcase is still more like a science experiment. Will everything fit? Will it weigh too much? Will I be able to repack it all? What do I do with these tiny, leftover, weird-shaped spaces that nothing fits in? Or worse, what if there's no space left, and I have more necessary things to take?

My emotional suitcase has been the same way—messy to pack and messy to unpack. So if you are like me, you may be thinking, *Unpack my emotional suitcase? Are you kidding?* It may seem daunting, but don't give up before you start.

God is a God of order and conviction but not condemnation. He is patient to wait and will only start working as we hand the suitcase over to Him. Perhaps you are in a lot of pain, and you just do not know where to begin. If so, start like I did—with a cry of desperation.

Get honest with God and with yourself. Admit your need for Him to gently lead you through the process, and start looking inward for cleansing, processing, and letting go.

Since we are all at a different place in this journey, there are no set rules to follow or formulas to make it "quick and painless." As I mentioned earlier, your heart surgery will be painful at times, but that doesn't mean the process is wrong or off track. When we experience pain, the intensity can stall the process if we allow it. I think of the Book of Psalms and King David when I think of stalling. I love the Psalms because they are the real, heartfelt expressions of a man who is trying to *process his pain*. David stalled regularly in working through his emotions, but he always came out with a firmer grasp on the faithfulness of God.

Many times while reading a psalm, I imagine David sitting and either dictating it to a scribe or writing the words himself. I can imagine that he might write a few sentences, get up, pace a bit, remind himself of truth, maybe pound his fists and talk out loud to God— being honest with God about his pain. Then I imagine him settling back down to write some more. Picturing him this way helps me see him processing the *trauma* and admitting the emotional pain associated with it. Then he concludes with truth and encourages himself about God, himself, and others. This is what I call *healthy processing*. You can learn this from the Psalms, too!

I have been unpacking for about 40 years, and even though I have not arrived (and won't be totally sanctified until death), God has done a great work in my soul. I would like to share some relevant principles to encourage you in your own unpacking process. I've distilled my list to three major principles I hold on to—sometimes for dear life!

Principle #1: Let God be your fishing guide.

Jesus was a master fisherman and gave His disciples precise instructions on where to let down their nets. Similarly, God knows what, in us, is "under the deep." He works beneath the surface and behind the scenes to arrange events, situations, and people in our lives and family to bring up what you need to unpack. You don't have to figure it out. God knows where to let down the nets. Your role is simply to be open and vigilant.

Some of your emotions have been stuffed for years, and it will take work to bring them to the surface. Frankly, some of the contents may be rather stinky, and you may feel some shame associated with them. And since you may have to address the emotions more than once (a lot more!), be encouraged. God will set a pace that's right for you. You just need to accept that God will do it in His order and in His timing. Be prepared to remind yourself of this over and over. Remember King David? He ran from King Saul for *ten years*, but God worked truth into his soul as he suffered and waited.

Principle #2: Don't judge luggage by its color.

As women, we have a tendency to compare our lives with other people's lives. We see the smiling faces at church, the obedient children as they walk respectfully with their parents, the husbands and wives who seem to enjoy one another, and we come to the automatic conclusion, "Wow! They have it all together, and I am a big failure!" I bought this lie many times until the Lord reminded me of an important truth a dear friend told me years ago: "You never know what goes on behind closed doors." Another way to say it is that you don't know what is in someone else's suitcase.

When traveling, I have stood by the luggage carousel looking at the different colored bags passing by. The most expensive ones are the most eye-catching and appealing, and many times I've said to myself, *I wonder what's in that suitcase. It looks so pretty and is probably filled with beautiful, expensive clothing.* But I really have no idea who is the owner of that beautiful suitcase, and I would no more trade someone else's luggage content for mine than I would trade my life for theirs. I have no idea what I would actually be getting.

Sometimes it's hard not to compare ourselves and our lives with others', but you can at least be realistic and honest—and dare I say *biblical*—about it. God has tailor-made our lives for each of us. He allows troubles, trials, and even trauma in this sinful world to enter our experiences, so His grace can enter into our experiences. *Everyone* has a story of heartbreak, disappointment, hurt, or injustice. For you to look on the outside and desire someone else's life because it seems carefree is not only a trick of the devil to deny God's good plan for you, but it keeps you distracted from focusing energy on your own suitcase. God has a *great plan* to someday exhibit each of us as trophies of His grace and mercy. We will be on display according to the measure of grace we have allowed Him to show us. So I encourage you to accept the plan God has for your life, believe He is in control, and know that all of your experiences are for a purpose.

God knows the contents of our stuffed souls. He was there when we stuffed them, and He will unpack them as we hand them over to Him. He knows exactly what we need to become aware of the contents, but since most of us are in the dark about what's inside, we need an in-your-face, present-day situation to reveal what is really in there. That's why He's put in us what I call an emotional magnet. This magnet causes us to be drawn into churches or marriages and into specific neighbor and in-law relationships. God then uses the interactions they foster and the inevitable conflicts that result to reveal our baggage. For most of us, marriage is the primary place this happens.

Have you ever wondered why a woman often marries a man whose personality is similar to one of her parents? Perhaps you've seen that in your own relationship. Ask yourself: *does my spouse remind me more of my dad or my mom?* Sometimes the connection is hidden at first, but how many times have you thought or said, "That reminds me of my dad (mom)," and it is not always a pleasant memory? God has used your inner magnet to attract you to a spouse who would eventually remind you of something the parent did or said. It may have been traumatic, and you stuffed it. Now God wants to use that present-day person to bring it out in the open so you can biblically process your suitcase. If something in your spouse is touching a nerve in you, it may be just what you need to identify some of your hidden, unprocessed emotions.

You may recall from science class that magnets not only attract but also can repel. I've seen this characteristic at work in my marriage, and it's not helpful. I remember a time I felt repulsed by Sam. He was returning from a weeklong missions trip to Haiti, and since we had no immediate family living nearby, I felt very much alone that week caring for our three small children. Sam got the message about my unhappiness the minute he stepped off the plane: I wasn't there. I had recruited a friend to take our children to the airport to meet him! I simply was not in the emotional frame of mind to greet him and knew I needed some serious help before he arrived home.

With the assistance of my counselor friend, I wrote out my feelings and realized that my emotions were fueled by the unprocessed feeling of abandonment I carried from childhood. I had so long believed the lie that I was not good enough for Sam to invest in emotionally that my lid finally blew. Eventually, I talked myself off the ledge by applying the truth that God will never leave me nor forsake me (Deuteronomy 31:6) and that a sovereign God unconditionally loves me. These truths from God's Word also kept me from throwing Sam "off the cliff" that day, when he stepped over the threshold.

Principle #3: God gives us "open-book" tests.

I am not very good test taker. I get anxious, confused, and easily overwhelmed. I never feel well prepared. I hesitate before answering and second guess my best guess. So test taking, for me, is very stressful.

But I love open-book tests! Nothing is better than hearing the teacher announce a test and follow up with these lifesaving words: "but you can use your book and your notes to take the test." Yes! That means I just have to familiarize myself with the information and develop a system to quickly find the answers. Wow! What a difference!

God is like that teacher. He has mercifully given us His Book to study, learn from, and pray through as we are in process. He not only gives us wisdom and answers but He also surrounds us with people who have gone before us and who can help us. He will faithfully use friends, pastors, authors, courses, and small group discussions to spur you on. You are not alone in this processing journey, and it is just another lie of your emotions if you feel isolated and think God is "out to get you." Your greatest ally is the supreme lover of your soul, God Himself. And the more intentionally you and your husband pray through God's Word together, the more life tests you will pass, individually, in your marriage, and in your family.

UNPACK AND PRAY

We often want to blame others for our misery and difficult emotions—in particular, we want to blame our husbands. Obviously, to the degree we blame them, we will have a harder time connecting with them in prayer. So if God uses husbands to aid in the unpacking process (as He did mine), we need to let Him. God is the surgeon who cuts deep into our emotions; He's the locksmith to unlock closets crammed with junky feelings; and He is the farmer who plows up hardened ground. At times, you will likely think your husband is the enemy, but God is using the closest person (or persons, if you have children) because, in order to unpack us, He needs to create the same emotional environment in which we packed in the first place.

When you have a physical infection, caused by trauma deep in your tissue, you need someone to expose it in order to apply the correct medication for healing. If you lose that perspective and blame, push away, withdraw, or shut down from your husband and family, you'll sacrifice the chance to have any intimacy at all—emotional, spiritual, or physical. Sadly, that is where many marriages and families are today. People blame, withdraw, accuse, distance, alienate, and divorce over some of the very things God is trying to use to draw attention to unhealthy, crammed souls. But your marriage doesn't have to be that way.

Will you trust and turn to the One who stood beside you as you packed your soul in ignorance and allow Him to be the One to help you as you deal with it—process it—toward healing? Only you can give Him permission to reveal what has been hidden for so long. And it is a huge step you can take to promote emotional and spiritual intimacy with your husband and family.

PRAY TOGETHER

*Make every effort to live in peace with everyone and to be
holy; without holiness no one will see the Lord. See to it
that no one falls short of the grace of God and that no bitter
root grows up to cause trouble and defile many.*

—HEBREWS 12:14–15

*Father in heaven, encourage and equip us to "make every effort
to live in peace with everyone." Although this is easy to pray, it can
be difficult to actually do. We realize, however, that we have personal
responsibility to be proactive in pursuing peace. In the atmosphere of
peace with You, with ourselves, and with one another, we can settle, in
calm, to thrive and grow in increasing holiness. Living with purity allows
us to "see the Lord" with more clarity and regularity. Help us, Lord, not
to miss Your grace. If a root of bitterness wraps around our hearts, we will
lack peace, and the result will be trouble and many people defiled. Comfort
and guide us in unpacking the emotional suitcases of our hearts that we
may become more like You. Amen.*

CHAPTER 8

INTIMACY AND THE HURDLES OF A MAN'S HEAD

(BY SAM)

I felt like the message was speaking directly to me, especially the part of feeling my wife, Teya, is more spiritual than me. I went and asked Teya for forgiveness for falling short in the area of praying with her. I told her what I desired to do, and she said this was an answer to her prayers. This is what she desired since we've been married. Two weeks in and we have been experiencing a love for God and one another stronger than ever before.

—DEANDRE

After 30 years of marriage, I would say Ruth and I were committed but dry and lacking hope. I believe most of our trouble is related to my poor leadership. I certainly lacked passion for both God and my wife. . . . I have begun to pray the Word with Ruth and sense that God is beginning to breath some fresh wind into our sails.

—STACY

A man sat on the front row at a men's breakfast seminar wearing a T-shirt with large writing on the front and back. The front said, "I'm not the man I ought to be . . ." And the back declared, "But thank God I'm not the man I used to be!" The T-shirt presents a statement of confession on the front and a declaration of hope on the back. And it resonates doesn't it? Clearly no one "arrives" this side of heaven.

I (Sam) imagine that with more resolve and obedience, each of us could be farther down the road toward maturity and pleasing God. Yet, on the other hand, hopefully we can look over our shoulder on this life journey and truly thank God that we are not where we used to be. We have experienced life and God; we have learned and grown; we are farther down the narrow way that befits the life of Jesus Christ in our individual lives and marriage. We have a measure of accomplishment and joy in gaining some ground. Yet we know there is a substantial—and perhaps daunting—journey still ahead.

HARDEST THING TO DO

Over the past several years, I have shared with many Christian men about the issue of spiritual intimacy in marriage, particularly dialing in on the issue of praying with our wives. I have also talked with most of my Christian male friends about the issue, and I have talked with all of the men in my extended family.

Frankly, many of these are godly men, involved in helping other people find and pursue a relationship with God. Among them are pastors, elders, deacons, seminary professors, ministry leaders, missionaries, Sunday School teachers, and ministry presidents. And when I ask the "do you pray with your wife" question, I have seen the facial expressions of men in the pews, at men's breakfasts, conferences, and seminars in the United States, Colombia, and Romania. Without exaggerating, I tell you the response has been virtually unanimous. At some level, every one of us carries a burden that we are not quite cutting it in spiritual intimacy in our marriage, and particularly concerning praying with our spouses.

A journey into any of our hearts, as men, would reveal unique backgrounds and a maze of experiences that have shaped who we are today. Beyond the psychological, emotional, family of origin, and other contributing factors, there is also a dark shield of spiritual resistance that seeks to block the efforts of Christian men. Spiritual opposition does not want any of us to step more intentionally into the role as the priest of the family.

This dark spirit invades the home, and if you and I don't get off the couch and confront the stranger attacking our homes, who is going to do it? Our wives? The children? Ha! Are we kidding ourselves? As men, we know we are designed to not only to be the family provider but also to be *protector* of our marriages and families. We're the ones who need to shove the stranger back out the front door!

NO BLUEPRINTS

In all my conversations with men, I've discovered a host of reasons why we abdicate responsibility in approaching our wives more regularly and intentionally for spiritual connectedness. Some of us did not experience the model of a spiritual husband and father in our families of origin—that was my situation.

Although I was raised in a *religious* home, it was not a *Christian* home, per se. My Dad was not a churchgoer when my brothers, sisters, and I were young. My parents required us kids to go to religious classes and church services, but they did not go with us to church very often. Dad worked hard six days a week at both full-time and multiple part-time jobs to provide for our large family, so he viewed Sunday as his personal time, and that was mostly occupied with hunting. As a result, I lacked modeling in my life of a spiritually engaged father.

Perhaps your spiritual heritage was similar. If so, you must still understand that this lack of good modeling does not let you off the hook. Now we are Christian husbands and fathers, and we must find a way to build spiritual homes with few, or no, blueprints to follow.

TWO HURDLES TO GET OVER

When I was in high school, I was quite a bit shorter than many of my classmates, but since I was pretty fast on my feet, I went out for the track team. Although I was far from being one of the team stars, by the end of the season, I had managed to earn woven numerals to sew on my high school jacket. I don't recall how it came about, but one of the events I ran was hurdles.

In running the hurdles, you not only had to sprint around the dark gravel track and stay in your lane, but you had to glide over a series of obstacles along the way. To vary the challenge (I suppose), there were two types of hurdle races: low hurdles and high hurdles. Short guy that I was, which hurdle race do you think I ran? Since the high hurdles came about up to my nose, I ran the low ones. I worked diligently on the right form for making it over a hurdle and did fine with the low ones, but the high ones? Forget it! It wasn't even worth trying. And that's what I've found most men think about genuine spiritual leadership. The hurdles are so high, they feel like quitting before they even start.

I have asked many men why they think this struggle is so common, and I've distilled their answers down to two high hurdles that seem to get in everyone's way.

Hurdle #1: Intimidation

The intimidation factor basically sounds like this: "My wife is ahead of me spiritually."

The truth is, many of us recognize that our wives are walking more diligently and intentionally with the Lord than we are. It intimidates us to think we might not have much to add to what she needs. And worse, we think we just might mess her up if we try! Men have said to me things like:

* "I am sure my wife loves Jesus more than I do!"
* "She reads the Bible more than I do."
* "She has a prayer partner, and they really know how to pray. Sometimes they pray for an hour or more at one sitting."
* "My wife is doing spiritually just fine without me."
* "Beyond our Sunday School class, she goes to another Bible study every week, and they even study the more unknown books in the Old Testament!"
* "I don't know what to do with her."
* "Should I teach her the Book of Ezekiel? But the problem is I don't know Ezekiel myself!"

Suppose you were to say to your wife, "OK, dear, the time has now come for you to sit at my feet, and I will string pearls of spiritual wisdom upon you from on high where I dwell." Along with my wife, your wife would say, "Really? I know where you dwell, buddy. Ain't goin' there." What's more, her response might be completely correct if you took that approach. And most of us know that.

If you feel your wife is ahead of you spiritually, guess what? Perhaps it's true. Maybe she is ahead of you. She may have known the Lord longer than you, she may seek to follow Him more intentionally, and she may be more diligent in spiritual disciplines.

God has blessed many of us with God-fearing wives, and the first thing we need to do is thank God for this reality. We should be saying, "Thank You, Lord, that You have chosen to yoke me with a woman who loves You!" Second, such a reality is no excuse to justify our lagging behind. God wants to use your wife's walk with Him to motivate your spiritual passion.

This was true in my life. God blessed me with Vicki, and she has been passionate, focused, and intentional about following Jesus Christ since she became a Christian in her late teenage years. Our encounters with the gospel of Jesus Christ came through radically different circumstances, and right from the beginning, Vicki was fully committed to giving her life to Christ and His service, but I was not so fast on the uptake.

Through our spiritual journey, the Lord showed me something that has been very freeing for me, and perhaps it will be for you, too. My wife does not need or desire for me to disciple her—especially if we think discipling means we are supposed to impart new spiritual information and fresh insights to her. Vicki has known the Lord for more than 40 years, knows the Bible well, and is a gifted prayer intercessor. If I try regularly to bring her new biblical ideas, I am going to run out of gas pretty quickly! It was a liberating day when I finally realized this is not what Vicki needs or even wants from me spiritually. She does not want me to teach her the Bible. She wants me to lead her spiritually.

For a long time, I was confused about what spiritual leadership really looks like in marriage. It does not mean we are more biblically astute than our wives. It does not mean we know more verses by memory than she does. It does not even mean that we impart distinctive spiritual information and insights to her. *Spiritually leading your wife is not information-centric; it is relationship-centric.* It involves walking in a relationship of three: husband, wife, and God. It is not about *how much you know* to impart to her. It is about *who you are* as her partner in life and your commitment to live yoked together with her—and with Jesus Christ. You are not supposed to be ahead, pulling her along. Nor are you are intended to push her from behind. You walk side-by-side in the realities of life. This includes the mountaintop blessings, the curses of deep, dark valleys, and everything in between. This way of walking will enhance your oneness, spiritual perspective, and emotional health.

Marriages are all over the map, but, generally, a wife desires her husband to come near her side in spiritual and emotional togetherness. When we do that, wives sense our love and attention to marriage, home, and family, possibly as never before. Although this may be difficult for you to receive, prayers with your wife matter more to her and to God than the prayers any other person may voice with her! You are her one-flesh partner in the covenant of marriage, and when you bow your heads and hearts before God in spiritual union, it makes a huge difference.

God created Eve from Adam's rib, not from the crown of his head, nor with the skin from the bottom of his foot. The rib came from Adam's side, and that image is quite revealing. God intends marriage to be a side-by-side, covenant relationship. Our wives are not intended to be under us or over us but beside us. *That* is Christian marriage.

So, men, let's leap over the high hurdle of intimidation. This hurdle kept me from fully assuming my marriage role with Vicki. Quite frankly, I still believe she is ahead of me in some dimensions of knowing and walking with God, but that is not the point. I seek to receive this reality in humility and accept it as a challenge to grow personally. Praying with my wife and using the Bible as a guide is a game changer. It raises me over the hurdle of intimidation and places us side by side in a stronger marital yoke.

Hurdle #2: Fear

We have been told since we were young that "real men are not afraid." Therefore, what man wants to admit he is afraid of something? But this second hurdle can cause us to shudder and hide because we remember, "My wife knows who I really am!" Men have said to me things like:

* ❖ "I got our family in terrible debt with more than one foolish decision."
* ❖ "My wife knows all my failures, shortcomings, and sins."
* ❖ "I lose my temper and yell at the kids pretty frequently."
* ❖ "I don't keep up with the chores around the house like I should."
* ❖ "I watch the wrong kind of movies, and my tongue gets pretty loose sometimes."
* ❖ "There is this ongoing argument with so-and-so that keeps coming up, and she knows I am actually racked with bitterness over the deal."

The list goes on and on, and our personal lists paralyze us with fear.

The fear hurdle condemns us because we are sinners and obviously your wife knows that. Given this reality, we know our wives will actually think badly of us if we try to come off as spiritual men. Imagine I just yelled at the kids and unfairly sent them all to bed. Then I am supposed to turn to my wife and say, "OK, honey, let's open the Bible to Proverbs and pray together"? Yeah, right! Drawing close to our wives spiritually and emotionally feels too revealing, shameful, and risky. Stepping into that much light brings too much exposure. We're almost certain to feel like hypocrites.

The usual answer is to avoid getting too close to our wives. Our condemnation and shame fuels our fear, so we blow the whistle and disqualify ourselves. Off to the penalty box we go. And we don't really have a plan for coming out. This leaves our wives and children to skate the ice alone. Certainly, we cannot win any games when we are confined in the penalty box!

So think about it: Who wants you in the penalty box? Your wife? Children? Perhaps your grandchildren? God? For that matter, do you really want to be there? None of the above. In fact, there's only one person anywhere who wants you in the penalty box. And who would that be? The devil! Yes, Satan wants to be sure you and I stay out of the action. The enemy uses our fallen nature to deal the condemning thoughts that persuade us to give up. And praying with our wives is the last thing we are drawn to do. We figure we are not good enough. But I have some news for you.

Newsflash #1: You are right. You're not good enough!

None of us will ever be *good enough* on our own merit. Period. So when would we ever be able to say, "OK, I am now good enough to pray with my wife"? How long would that take?

Approaching God is not about our self-righteousness qualifying us for the meeting. As Isaiah 64:6 says, "All of us have become like one who is unclean, and all our righteous acts are like filthy rags; we all shrivel up like a leaf, and like the wind our sins sweep us away." And the New Testament offers about the same assessment: "There is no one righteous, not even one" (Romans 3:10). But God, in His grace, has the solution for our sin crisis. He provided a substitute to take the death penalty we deserved: His one and only Son, the Lord Jesus Christ. Isaiah 53:6 declares, "We all, like sheep, have gone astray, each of us has turned to our own way; and the LORD has laid on him the iniquity of us all."

Thank God for allowing us the Great Exchange: "God made Him who had no sin to be sin for us, so that in him we might become the righteousness of God" (2 Corinthians 5:21). This is the heart of the gospel. God laid upon Jesus our sin debt and, in exchange, gave us His righteousness. Only this righteousness of Jesus Christ qualifies us for eternal salvation. Likewise, our qualification to come before God in prayer is not because of who we are but because of who we are in His Son Jesus Christ.

This means you are not disqualified from praying with your wife. Unworthy? Yes! But disqualified? No! (And remember: no matter how highly you regard your wife, her own righteousness doesn't make her "good enough" either!)

My brother, none of us is perfect, but consider this: the answers, motivations, and healings we need can flow from the Word of God as we pray through the truths and principles of Scripture. The most powerful relational union that God intends on earth is husband and wife. No other relationship is characterized by such intimate and personal terms as "one flesh." When you invite the living God to reside at the center of your marriage, you have access to His life in a unique way. Stepping into this union more intentionally and regularly will open the anointing of God in ways you may not have imagined. On the other hand, if you step back from the power resident in such a union of prayer, you lose access to the most powerful resource you have as a married man.

Once while I was leading a men's meeting about this issue of praying the Word in marriage, Vicki observed from the back of the room. At the end of the main talk, the group moved into a question and answer time, and this issue of men feeling disqualified came up.

I shared some of the same thoughts I offered in this chapter, and one of the men had the boldness to ask, "Hey, what does Vicki think about this issue?"

At first I could tell she was hesitant to talk to an entire room filled with men, but her response hit the nail right on the head! She said, "Yes, men, your wives know who you are. She probably knows you better than you know yourself. She knows what you will do and what you will not do. She knows how you are going to react to situations. . . . She is your wife!

"I would say there are probably two things she really longs to see in your life: honesty and humility. She is not impressed with faking or hiding. She wants you to be honest with yourself, her, and God. And this is related to humility, of course. If you come near her spiritually, with some honesty and humility, odds are very good that it will touch and soften her heart."

You could have heard a pin drop in the room. God spoke through Vicki to the bull's-eye of all of our hearts.

Think about the power of Vicki's counsel to that room of Christian husbands and fathers. What two sins frequently trip us up as men: dishonesty, which is the opposite of honesty, and pride, which is the opposite of humility.

Ironically, we think we are being dishonest if we come out of the penalty box, but that is not the case. The truth is, by staying in, we are surrendering to abdication, abandoning our post. Instead, boldly embracing honesty and humility compels us to exit the penalty box. So, get out. Refuse to go back! Based on who you are in Jesus Christ and upon the authority of God's Holy Word, kick open the penalty box and come back out on the ice. Your wife, children, and God will welcome you!

Newsflash #2: The thief comes only to steal, kill, and destroy.

One evening after returning home from a meeting, I sat on the couch in our living room looking over some emails. Vicki was in another room, at the back of the house, when a blurry image caught my attention on the other side of the frosted glass in the front door. Someone was approaching! I thought it must be one of our adult daughters coming over to visit, but as the image stepped onto our front porch, I realized this person was too large to be one of our girls. In fact, it looked like a man—a sizable man!

This all happened in just a few seconds. I expected the doorbell to ring or a knock to sound, but instead, the front door opened, and a stranger stepped across the threshold! I jumped off the couch, dashed across the living room to meet the guy, and placed my outstretched hand solidly on his chest.

"Whoa, man, what are you doing?"

I am all for hospitality, but this intrusion was not befitting a warm welcome by any stretch of the imagination—especially not for this burly twentysomething! He was wearing earphones and held an iPod in his hand, and when I jolted him to a halt, he looked stunned. His eyes darted from side to side.

"Oh man, I guess I'm in the wrong house!"

Noting the look on his face and hearing his slurred speech, I instantly realized this guy was out of it, high on something. Before I could say another word, he backpedaled out the front door. Although in retrospect I am not sure I did the right thing, I stepped out on the porch behind him and firmly told him that he had, in fact, walked into the wrong house and that I did not appreciate it. Thankfully, the immediate encounter ended with that. He turned and stumbled down the sidewalk away from my house, but by that time, Vicki showed up. As I told her what had just happened, she turned a bit pale. The young man, though, continued to ramble around in the street, so I decided it was time to call the police. They showed up in short order, ended up cuffing the guy, and took him to the station for public drunkenness and disorderly conduct.

The whole incident was a bit unsettling, to say the least. I could only imagine what might have happened had I not been home. What if this guy had happened upon Vicki inside our house? It certainly reinforced the lesson that we needed to keep our front door locked, even though we live in a normally quiet community.

This story also reminds me that there is another who desires to enter our homes unwelcomed. He is the thief Jesus warns about in John 10:10, saying, "The thief comes only to steal and kill and destroy."

Jesus refers to the devil as a *thief*, a murderous, destructive thief. His schemes are always designed to take away what is best from us and our families. That is his *only* agenda.

When the enemy convinces you that you are disqualified from praying with your wife, he tricks you into stepping away from one of the most powerful resources you have in your life: one-flesh, spiritual intimacy. With this subtle scheme, he steals, kills, and destroys vast fruitfulness from your life and family. But the devil is disarmed when we fight with the Word of God. This is the same strategy Jesus used against Satan during His temptations in the wilderness.

So imagine: if you knew a literal thief was coming to your home to ravage your wife, harm your children, and steal your things, you would rise to the occasion and resist him with all your power. Well, gentlemen, *the thief is at hand!* Most often he does not come crashing in loudly and forcefully. More commonly, he works slowly, robbing God of His glory and taking joy from your marriage and family.

PROTECT YOUR FAMILY WITH PRAYER

Do not allow the enemy to shame you into opting out of the most powerful resource in your life and marriage. Determine to step up to your role as spiritual leader. By praying the Bible with your wife, you will be equipped to fight the good fight as never before. The heart of a husband and father innately beats with a commitment to provide for and protect his wife and children.

This is the core of the challenge we address in this book. In our generation, marriage and family are under severe attack. It is a war for the souls of our children. The thief especially targets children, teens, and young adults. As fathers, you and I have the responsibility not only to protect them as best we can physically but spiritually as well. Can you think of a better way to cover your family spiritually than to pray over them a consistent diet of God's living Word?

A MOVEMENT OF CHRISTIAN MEN

The vast majority of Christian men truly do desire to be spiritual leaders in their homes. Yet we often don't know how to make that happen. We try taking our families to church. We get them involved in multiple church activities and programs. But we still sense something is missing at a more personal level of spiritual interaction and influence in our marriages and family life. Praying through the Bible, though, makes *the* difference because you know where you are headed together in prayers. And that's just what most men need.

I've already talked about the basic reasons not to wait until you "feel worthy," but the process itself will improve your spiritual life.

The growing answers and resources for your life and your family are found in the journey. Sometimes, I know, we wish God would "show up" first. Then we could move forward with confidence. But the kingdom of God normally works in paradox—the opposite of our natural way of thinking. The way His kingdom operates is that He wants us to trust Him and press forward by faith. *Then* He shows up.

One other really cool thing about what's happening among Christian men these days is that, if you take the step of initiating Bible-led prayer with your wife, you won't be alone. You probably hear about many different "movements" arising in our world. There are movements to influence politicians, movements in the medical community to cure chronic illnesses, movements within the missions community. But what movement could powerfully influence marriages, families, the church, and our society at a most profound and transformational level? It is the very movement you step into when you initiate the *Praying Together* kind of spiritual intimacy with your wife. It's a movement of husbands who have the courage to make a twofold resolution before God and their wives:

> (1) Resolve to step into God's design as the spiritual leader of your marriage and family by initiating one-flesh spiritual intimacy with your wife, demonstrated by praying together on a regular basis.

> (2) Resolve to use the Bible as the guide and template for the content, topics, and flow for your prayers.

And how do I know this movement exists? Because I've seen it with my own two eyes—all over the world.

FOR YOUNG AND OLD ALIKE

Virtually every time I share this story with a friend, it pains me to realize I have lost so much time in my own life. If you are a young husband (I'm not any more), I beg you as a brother ahead of you in the journey of life: do not continue along as you are and ultimately find yourself with the pain of having failed your wife and family by lack of leadership in prayer. Seize the opportunity now! Catch the vision today! Take the step of providing a one-flesh spiritual umbrella to cover your marriage, family, and ministry. Pour God's Word over your family—its principles, values, and truths. The potential fruitfulness in the lives of your children alone is far, far worth it. And if you find yourself with a wayward child someday, as Vicki and I did, you will know you did all you could to provide a covering of the Word of God over his or her soul. And the good news in such a situation is: His Word will not return void. We saw this happen in our daughter Christina's life in an amazing way.

If you are an older husband, you may have a string of marital years already under your belt. God's alarm has been ringing in your life, and you have been hitting the snooze button over and over. You have lost much time—as I had. I want to remind you of a spectacular truth of God's kingdom economy: God is able to restore the years the locusts have eaten. He makes all things work together for the good of those who love Him, who have been called according to His purpose (Romans 8:28). That includes even our losses, which God can transform to become productive in His kingdom and in our lives.

IS THIS THE APPOINTED TIME FOR YOU?

Your choice to do this or not is potentially a life-transforming decision. I also believe it is not a decision you make on your own.

A resolve of this significance is one you cannot embrace apart from the conviction that God is calling you to do it. Remember in Chapter 2, we talked about Habakkuk 2:3, where the prophet says the "revelation awaits an appointed time"? It brings me to a question I must ask: is this the appointed time for you?

All that Vicki and I have said so far might seem reasonable, rational, and *biblical*. But does it grip you? Is it compelling? Do you sense the Lord calling you to answer an alarm that has been ringing in your life, maybe for a long time?

If so, unload your burden!

Scores of Christian men live with the burden of knowing they are failing in spiritual leadership at home. They work on it from time to time, but it doesn't seem to take hold and last.

You may be doing well at church, on the elder or deacon board, on the church staff, in teaching Sunday School, and in other aspects of Christian life and service. Then, from time to time, you hear a message or sermon that convicts you about your lack of spiritual leadership at home. And you feel guilty! You ride home in silence, the burden increased even more. But perhaps now God is giving you a clear revelation.

Gentlemen, there is a simple solution right in front of us. In fact, it is so right in front of us that I am amazed I missed it for so long in my own marriage. But now that has changed. The truth is I am feeling *much* better about this part of my marriage and spiritual leadership. I might even dare to say I feel *good* about it! Not only is Vicki experiencing blessing and love in a fresh way, I, too, am deeply enjoying what the Lord has done in our marriage and spiritual life together. I truly miss it when, for some reason, we are not able to have our prayertime together. We learn wonderful truths from the Bible and see God bring life and answers to multiple concerns in our lives, family, and ministry. The fingerprints of God have been evident—and we are praising Him for the transformation!

SOME HELPFUL TIPS

1. Apologize . . . really?

If you want to get out of the penalty box, the first step you must take is to tell your wife about the revelation you have received. Tell her about your new commitment that has come to you by God's grace. It could be that you owe your wife an apology for lost time. And bear in mind that a true apology does not just express sorrow. You also need to ask for her forgiveness.

Forgiveness is offered once repentance is demonstrated. In other words, repentance lived out over a reasonable time opens the door to reconciliation and forgiveness. She needs to see that your apology has substance. Behavior change over time puts the skin on an apology.

Vicki did not say so, but I'm fairly certain there was some skepticism in a corner of her heart when I made my apology. That may happen in your situation as well (imagine your wife's arms crossed as she says, "OK, we'll see what happens"). If so, it simply means you and I need to live out our resolve. One friend shared with me that, when he apologized to his wife for his previous lack of spiritual leadership, she said to him, "You have no idea how much your apology means to me!" His acknowledgment and confession touched her heart more than he would have ever anticipated.

2. Ladies First

This is not a rule, per se, but generally speaking, I prefer that my wife go first in sharing what she observes in the verses we read in our prayertimes. I often say, "Honey, what jumps out at you?" This is a great time to listen to your wife's heart—an opportunity for you to understand how God is speaking to her. When we offer spiritual and emotional attention, our wives find increased peace and joy. It tells her that you seek to love her as Christ loved the Church (Ephesians 5:25).

3. Journey with Other Men

A friend sent me this email: "I know, for me, if I hear a challenge like this, and I say to myself, 'I'm in,' it may or may not last. However, if I tell someone else 'I'm in,' then I will have a brother that I will also be accountable to."

He is right on the mark! A crucial part of this decision is to journey together with other men who share the same resolve. You are primarily accountable to God and your wife, of course, but other men can offer much-needed support. Your wife will know if you follow through or not, but you do not want her to be in the position of holding your feet to the fire. You need other men to do that—others who are also committed to the journey.

Doing this with a friend or a group of men is a huge asset for your resolve. I have no idea how you came across this book, but perhaps if a friend recommended it, he would be a suitable accountability partner. Wherever you find the right person, though, please find someone. Do not embark on this path alone. You need other married men to co-own the resolve.

I do not advocate an overbearing system of checking up on one another, however. Such efforts only produce a legalistic and rote following, and it fails the very spirit of what we are seeking in a genuine spiritual walk with God and our wives. You don't need another thing to check off your to-do list, just so you can say, "I did it." What each of us needs is a band of "mighty men" who seek to be powerful in the economy of God's kingdom. We need a friend, or several friends, who can help us through the realities of life, who will pray for us as we pray for them. Hebrews 10:24-25 affirms this:

> *And let us consider how we may spur one another on toward love and good deeds, not giving up meeting together, as some are in the habit of doing, but encouraging one another—and all the more as you see the Day approaching.*

Not long ago, I shared this challenge with a gathering of men on a Saturday morning at a local church. At the conclusion, I asked the men to simply put their name, email address, and wife's name on a notecard if they felt led to step toward the marriage prayer journey. Suddenly, a man stood up and walked forward and handed me his notecard. He then turned to his Christian brothers and said, "Men, I needed to hear this challenge! I also know I need to be held accountable. So I am going to write my name on the whiteboard, and if you want to be held accountable as well, you, too, come write your name."

From that moment, during our closing prayer, and continuing afterwards, man after man, made his way forward to pen his name publicly. It was a brave gesture by that first man. But he "got it," and he stepped forward to the call for commitment. He knew the only way he would succeed was if he could journey together, not only with his wife but also with a band of like-minded brothers.

It is not good to go it alone. Over and over, the Bible tells of God sending men forward, not only with His presence, but side by side with other men. We can encourage each other in the spiritual battle.

Think about who you can influence to press into more intentional and regular spiritual leadership in his marriage. Can you think of the name of another believing husband you know needs to hear this challenge? Can you come up with three to five friends who are Christian husbands? How about ten others? How about other husbands in your own extended family? These are all potentially the men with whom you can journey so as to encourage one another.

4. If Your Wife Doesn't Want to Pray with You

Perhaps this whole discussion is painful to you because your marriage is in a difficult place. Maybe your wife will not agree to pray through the Bible with you. If that's the case, then I call you to press into the Lord even more deliberately. You can follow this approach on your own. In fact, there is nothing better you can do in the midst of such a challenge than to pray the Word of God for your wife, your family, and for yourself.

Because of who you are in her life, you can pray more effectively for your wife than anyone else. You might have a hard time believing that, but it is true.

If your wife is resistant, there may be a host of complex issues creating this condition in her heart. You need to consider seriously what responsibility you bear for your wife's condition. Ask God to show you. Even better, ask God for the boldness and right opportunity to ask your wife how you may have wounded her. If you have crushed her in some way, ask God to show His path to reconciliation and healing.

Are you willing to do whatever you can do to bring health and wholeness to your marriage? It will likely not be an easy path, but it will be well worth the trouble in the long run.

DOES THIS REALLY MATTER?

If you and your wife were to pray the Word and will of God over your children and/or grandchildren, do you think it would matter? If you are a Christian, it seems to me your answer should be "yes." Because if your answer is, "no, it probably doesn't matter," then you should just walk away from all this foolishness. You need to come to grips with your basic belief in the power of prayer.

Do you believe it can make a difference if you step up and step in intentionally and regularly to connect spiritually with your wife? Will it matter if you come out of the penalty box? Do you believe prayer is really talking to the God of all eternity and creation? When you pray, do you really know you are communicating personally with the same God who created the universe, who burned in the bush before Moses, who opened the Red Sea? Because you are! He is able to make a difference when you pray, and He wants to show up in your marriage.

PRAY TOGETHER

Husbands, in the same way be considerate as you live with your wives, and treat them with respect as the weaker partner and as heirs with you of the gracious gift of life, so that nothing will hinder your prayers.

—1 PETER 3:7

Lord, I thank You for my wife. I recognize I need to take this verse to heart, so I ask You to fill me with Your love to live with my wife in a considerate manner. I desire to treat her with respect, recognizing that she is a fellow heir of the gracious gift of life, which comes from You, so nothing will hinder my prayers and our prayers together. Grant me the faith and resolve to step over the hurdles of intimidation and fear as I learn to pray Your Word with my wife. Amen.

SEVEN BENEFITS OF PRAYING THE BIBLE

I was leading the church weekly but didn't quite know how to step out in leadership for my wife. Erin and I were always "happy" in our marriage but often lacked the spiritual connection as a couple. Praying through the Scriptures has transformed how we pray and often what we pray. It's opened the door for great spiritual conversation between the two of us and even made God's Word come alive in fresh ways. She and I are unified like never been before. Funny, it's not rocket science, but the simple act of letting the Scripture lead makes all the difference.

—PASTOR STEVE

I've been in full-time ministry (youth and men's ministry) for five years, part-time for three before that. I'm also in my last semester of seminary. Like so many others I have struggled to consistently lead my wife in prayer throughout our nine years of marriage. I came across your materials and loved them. It has transformed our prayer life together. We are keeping a journal as we go along. We read a brief passage, talk about it, and then each share three prayer requests. It has really improved my personal prayer life as well.

—BRIAN

One of the most solemn and mysterious scenes in the Bible occurs in a garden. It was called Gethsemane, and the story takes place the night before Jesus went to the Cross on Calvary.

> *Then Jesus went with his disciples to a place called Gethsemane, and he said to them, "Sit here while I go over there and pray."*
>
> —MATTHEW 26:36

Then,

> *Going a little farther, he fell with his face to the ground and prayed, "My Father, if it is possible, may this cup be taken from me. Yet not as I will, but as you will." Then he returned to his disciples and found them sleeping.*
>
> —vv. 39–40

Sleeping? Here they are with Jesus—supposedly His most devoted followers—at this utterly climactic moment of His life, and what are they doing? They're sleeping! And this happens not once, or twice, but three times. Each time, Jesus returns to find His closest followers in slumberland. Great prayer partners, huh? Jesus seemed compassionate with their weakness, though, because His only comment was, "The spirit is willing, but the flesh is weak" (v. 41).

It's easy to read that story and think the disciples were real wimps that night, but if we had been there, I wonder if we really would have done any better. After all, when is last time you spent a whole hour praying, let alone in the middle of the night? It often seems like we run out of things to pray about in only a few minutes, doesn't it? Focused prayer takes discipline.

A DISCIPLE'S DISCIPLINE

Therefore, putting aside all malice and all deceit and hypocrisy and envy and all slander, like newborn babies, long for the pure milk of the word, so that by it you may grow in respect to salvation, if you have tasted the kindness of the Lord.

—1 PETER 2:1–3, NASB

Long after that night in the garden, Peter wrote to his followers and obviously had learned a lot. Babies long for milk, he told them, drawing an analogy to the richness of how God supplies what we need for spiritual growth.

For a newborn baby, milk is the sole source of nourishment for physical growth. In ancient days, this life-sustaining milk was available only at the mother's breast. One of the most tender and serene images is a newborn held close in the security of his or her mother's embrace. Babies don't just desire milk because they like the taste. They long for it because they so desperately need it. And the wonderful result of consuming milk is . . . growth. The thirst for milk is motivated by hunger and desire is normal and healthy. In fact, a *lack* of longing for it signals that something is wrong.

Peter uses this timeless analogy to teach us an important lesson. Christians are supposed to long for the pure milk of the Word. This longing to feed our souls and spirits is evidence that we have tasted the kindness of the Lord—and we know it's good! The milk of the Word is our nourishing, life-sustaining resource for growing in Christ.

The Holy Spirit stirs a holy hunger within our hearts, and it is more than mere desire. It is a deep longing. And like a newborn baby, the longing is normal. Spiritual hunger signals health in the believer.

God desires that we grow spiritually strong as His children, but without His milk, we cannot grow. Without it, we will be overcome with weakness and be vulnerable to all manner of temptations and evil.

Healthy believers in Jesus Christ pursue a variety of disciplines that give us opportunities to drink in the milk of the Word. A diet of regular personal Bible reading, for instance, is important. Reading with our spiritual antennae raised, we can contemplate the meaning of Scripture. This is the discipline of meditation, and through it, we discern what the Spirit of God is speaking into our lives.

Another level of drinking God's milk is to *study* the Word. This requires a more intentional effort to dig for deeper observations, interpretations, and applications. What is God saying? What does it mean? How can I apply this to my life? When you study, you are not merely acquiring knowledge of spiritual things but are also hearing personally from God, it is the way to build your life on the rock foundation of obedience.

James challenges believers to not only hear the Word, but to be doers of the Word (James 1:22). This includes sharing with other people what God is showing us and how He is working in our lives. In so doing, we share the milk with other thirsty, hungry people, and it's good for both them and us.

Yet another means for ingesting milk is memorizing verses—even whole passages—from the Scriptures. With memorization, the nourishing Word not only passes through our minds but is ingrained in *us*. When committed to memory, the words literally become part of us. In this way, we arm our minds with truth, so we can call the Word into our circumstances at any time.

Each one of these disciplines is vital in our Christian walk and help us mature in salvation. Praying the Word brings them all together in a special way that provides both internal and external benefits for your marriage.

SWORD OF THE SPIRIT

Two other passages illustrate the Word in a very different way. These liken Scripture to a sword, and the imagery was especially powerful to first-century readers. The Roman short sword was the most common handheld weapon of the first century, and skillful use of this weapon made the person wielding it an effective offensive force in battle. A passage from Hebrews uses the analogy this way:

> *For the word of God is alive and active. Sharper than any double-edged sword, it penetrates even to dividing soul and spirit, joints and marrow; it judges the thoughts and attitudes of the heart.*
>
> —HEBREWS 4:12

This passage reflects the internal impact of the Word. The Word penetrates—goes inside of—a person's soul and spirit. It judges our thoughts and the attitudes of our hearts.

As we are imbued with the Word, God increasingly claims territory in our souls, minds, wills, and emotions. Through the Word of God, the Holy Spirit interacts with us in a deeply personal way.

The other passage likening the Bible to a sword is Ephesians 6. Under house arrest in Rome, the Apostle Paul is undoubtedly guarded by Roman foot soldiers, so naturally, in his letter to the church in Ephesus, Paul constructs a spiritual parallel of the Christian "soldier" to a Roman soldier. He knows we face enemies in life and says,

Finally, be strong in the Lord and in his mighty power.
Put on the full armor of God, so that you can take your
stand against the devil's schemes.

—EPHESIANS 6:10–11

Our opponents cannot be seen with the human eye. They consist of spiritual forces of wickedness that reside and work from the heavenly realms. Fighting them requires a complete set of armor that Paul refers to as the belt of truth, breastplate of righteousness, gospel of peace, shield of faith, and helmet of salvation. But the final, essential element for the well-prepared soldier is his sword—"the sword of the Spirit, which is the word of God," according to Paul in Ephesians 6:17. It's the sword that allows us to engage in spiritual combat and to go on the offensive against the enemy of our individual lives, our marriages, and our children.

PRAYING THE WORD, INSIDE AND OUT

Praying the Word makes the sword more effective *within us* (the internal effect) and increasingly *useful by us* (the external impact).

When we pray the Word, the Holy Spirit stirs within us in a special and personal manner. While we would not presume to prioritize the importance or effectiveness of the various disciplines for engaging the word, we would say that adding praying the Word to your "spiritual activities" list will deepen your experience of God. When we pray the Word, it is woven into our souls. Our spiritual sight is sharpened. Our minds renewed. Our emotions are stabilized, and our wills increasingly surrendered. Praying Scripture brings God's values, promises, blessings, truths, doctrines, praises, and much more into our souls. The double-edged sword becomes a razor sharp surgical tool in the hands of the Great Physician. He slices into the thoughts and intents of our heart and renews us in all the inner thoughts and emotions (suitcases) that need renewing. He highlights commands we need to obey, sins we need to confess, promises we need to claim, blessings we need to receive, and praises we need to offer. It's the best way we've found to vividly experience Paul's exhortation to the Christians in Colosse, when He wrote, "Let the message of Christ dwell among you richly as you teach and admonish one another with all wisdom through psalms, hymns, and songs from the Spirit, singing to God with gratitude in your hearts" (Colossians 3:16).

There is also an external impact in the realm of spiritual battle when we pray the Word. We are encouraged and fortified to stand firm in the spiritual battle the devil brings to our doorstep. The rulers, authorities, and powers of the dark world are as real as the things we view with our physical eyes, and their goal is to destroy our lives, marriages, families, and, ultimately, the Church of Jesus Christ. While we do not believe there is a demon behind every trouble and trial that we face in our lives, we do believe that spiritual opponents are real and that a fallen angel named Satan leads them. Jesus Himself faced the devil in the wilderness during His season of temptation (see Matthew 4:1-11), and in John 10:10, Jesus warns His flock that "the thief comes *only* to steal and kill and destroy" (authors' emphasis).

SEVEN BENEFITS OF PRAYING THE WORD AS HUSBAND AND WIFE

The theology and practice of prayer is shrouded in considerable mystery. God is sovereign and knows all things, and yet God's people are clearly called to pray to Him. Based on the authority of God's Word, the specific model and commands of Jesus Christ, and from our own experience with God, we know prayer is an essential and significant aspect of a healthy Christian walk. We also know that it is quite common to feel inadequate in the ministry of prayer. At times, we still struggle in our personal prayer lives—and in praying together as husband and wife. As a result, we've come to know well the need for encouragement to continue. We welcome practical help for enhancing our prayer lives and have noted, over time, the distinct benefits that accrue to us and our family when we do manage to stay on the prayer track. Perhaps our list of the top seven benefits we have found in praying the Bible will encourage you, too.

1. Guided Prayers

When we pray off the top of our heads, we tend to pray about the same things, mostly in the same manner. We struggle with what to say and feel limited in the scope of our prayers. Some people seem to be better at praying than others. They are comfortable with words and when they pray, there is a sense that God is in the room. However, most of us don't feel creative enough nor spiritual enough, to sweep the heavens with all manner of eloquent intercessions and praises. We simply don't know what to pray! After a few lines, we have run out of gas. Sometimes, even we, Sam and Vicki, feel like we're back in the prayer groups early in our walk with God, hoping no one asks us to pray out loud!

Having a prayer guide is one of the greatest benefits of following the Bible in our prayers. We never lack for ideas to fill our prayers. Whatever the Bible is talking about in a given passage becomes the day's prayer topic. Guided by the Holy Spirit, our prayers become as fresh as the flow of God's Word.

The guide also helps keep our minds on track. Perhaps like us, you've noticed that there are times in the middle of praying that our minds tend to "wander off." The day's to-do list drifts to the forefront, last night's movie comes to mind, or planning the weekend menu suddenly becomes crucial. But with the Bible providing the content for our prayers, mental drift is cut short because we have a tool to keep us focused.

Guided prayer highlights issues on our hearts, which the Bible helps us express in a more intimate way. Instead of our prayers "bouncing off the ceiling," we know we are praying the things that are on the heart of God. We can enjoy a connection with our spouses and with the Lord in prayer, possibly as never before.

2. Alignment: On the Same Page with the Holy Spirit

One thing for sure can be said about husbands and wives, and that is, they are different. We are different in gender, strengths, gifts, tastes, desires, talents, and perspectives—basically, in just about every way under the sun! And although it may seem ironic, these very differences are often the things that attracted us to our spouses in the first place. As the journey of real life unfolds, though, the differences that enhanced our romance in the beginning can become sources of friction and even serious troubles. It becomes more difficult to remember that the differences are, many times, a gift from God meant to bless rather than "curse" our relationship. That's why we need help staying in alignment with each other. The more aligned you are on the path of life with your spouse, the more you will experience peace in your marriage, family, child-rearing, finances, in-laws, sexual relations, and more.

Spiritual alignment touches every dimension of marriage. The Apostle James says, "Come near to God and he will come near to you" (James 4:8), and this principle is not just meant for us as individual believers but also for our marriages. Spiritual intimacy as a couple brings us more into alignment with God and one another.

Being properly aligned affects how we see God and each other. Years ago, the Lord gave us a clear but difficult lesson in how this works. As a young child, our daughter Christina suffered from a crossed right eye. This affected many aspects of her ability to see correctly. Clarity of vision, depth perception, and peripheral vision are achieved only when our eyes are working together, so Christina had a problem. Muscles controlling the movement of her eye just weren't doing their job, and she had to endure double vision. Time, eye exercises, and patching did not solve the problem, so, finally, when she was only five years old, she needed surgery. We lived in northern New Jersey at the time, so we availed ourselves of the best surgeon we could find in New York City. We were committed to whatever sacrifices it would require to see that Christina's eyes would work together in alignment, and, thankfully, the surgery was a success.

As husband and wife, we need to constantly adjust our alignment with one another, so we can see straight spiritually. Praying the Word is the regular intervention we need for the health of our spiritual eyes and for walking in the blessing that our differences complement each other, and do not get in the way of intimacy.

3. Strength for Facing the Realities of Life

One of the things that makes playing card games entertaining is that you are constantly encountering new cards as the game progresses. Sometimes the cards you get add fun to the game, but other times, they're downright frustrating. Kind of reminds you of life, doesn't it? You can't control which cards are dealt to you. You can only manage them once they're in your hand. Sometimes we draw cards that perfectly fit into a hand, but other times, we draw terrible cards and have no idea where to place them. An unexpected card can mess up our entire plan for winning the game! And often, there is no way to discard it. You can't control which cards are dealt to you. You can only manage them once they're in your hand.

We praise God because we have been dealt and have drawn many wonderful, blessed cards in our lives. However, just like you, we have also encountered many difficult cards over the decades we've been together. Life is very *real*. The cards that bless or mess our hands come in a wide variety: financial cards, health cards, emotional cards, relationship and child-rearing cards, career-change cards, moving cards—piles and piles of cards. As we write this, we are praying for several dear friends who are trying to manage seriously life-altering cards in their lives. And there's plenty of material in the Bible to help.

Almost 400 times, Scripture uses the words strong and strength. The Word of God is a source of strength. In his first epistle, John says, "I write to you, fathers, because you know him who is from the beginning. I write to you, young men, because you are strong, and the word of God abides in you, and you have overcome the evil one" (1 John 2:14 ESV). The source of spiritual strength is the Word of God.

Praying the Word of God strengthens us for facing the realities of life together. It provides the wisdom we need to know how to play the cards in our life-hand. It reinforces us for the inevitable storms and positions us to overcome the evil one.

4. Covering of Protection

A request for protection is something we frequently voice in our prayers. The inclination to pray for safety, security, and sheltering arises naturally from our hearts. While we know God is sovereign—

He knows all things and is in charge of our lives—we still realize intuitively, and from our experiences, that we live in hostile territory.

Even the Lord's Prayer in Matthew 6:9-13 reminds us to pray for protection:

> *Our Father in heaven, hallowed be your name, your king-dom come, your will be done, on earth as it is in heaven. Give us today our daily bread. And forgive us our debts, as we also have forgiven our debtors. And lead us not into temptation, but* deliver us from the evil one. *(authors' emphasis)*

So, praying for protection is appropriate and important. Concerning this particular benefit of praying the Word of God, however, we want to focus on praying over our children and grandchildren. Having talked to countless Christians about praying the Word in their marriages, this is one of the most attention-arresting issues that strikes the hearts of Christian parents and grandparents.

We were at a store recently and noticed a bin of umbrellas for sale. These were not small umbrellas—the kind that allow you to end up wet around the edges—these were massive, broad, overarching umbrellas big enough to cover a whole family. Umbrellas like these create a covering that provides the comfort of staying dry and prevents us from becoming soaked by rainwater.

Now think of your marriage as an umbrella. Husband and wife are joined together, and their marriage is intended to provide protection for the whole family. Praying the Word is like popping open a broad spiritual umbrella over your family. You provide blessings, promises, truths, virtues, values, teachings, praises, and intercessions from God's Word that impact the lives of your children and grandchildren.

There is nothing more important you could do for them! And you are potentially protecting them from some things far more damaging than rainwater. We mentioned earlier that the thief comes to steal, kill, and destroy. Our children are precious to each of us, but the evil one does not care. He is out to steal them from God, to destroy them.

Ephesians 6 talks of the fiery darts that Satan flings at our lives. He's also flinging them at our children and grandchildren. We believe it is more challenging to raise godly children in this modern generation than ever before. When we grew up in the Midwest, it was the days when you shouted to your mom as you ran out the door that you were going to the park to play. And if you didn't come home till dusk, nobody worried. But what responsible parent today would send their children off to a local park without supervision? And the threats are not only outside the home. Now they storm in through the media that batters young minds and hearts.

Our job as parents includes praying for the generation of lives that God has entrusted to our stewardship. We don't recall any of our daughters coming from the womb with a certificate of guarantee that everything would work out the way we hoped, but we can shift "the odds" in their favor with our prayers. Our children and grandchildren must face the cards of their own lives as they grow and mature, make decisions, and face the attendant consequences. In time, they will need their own faith and walk with God and not live off the faith of their parents and grandparents.

So, do you really *believe it matters if you pray for your children and grandchildren?* Pause, ask yourself that question, and answer it honestly. Hopefully, your answer is a resounding "Yes!" We would guess that if you've read this far, that is, indeed, your answer.

So, given your affirmative answer, it begs the next question: *are you praying for your children and grandchildren?* Not the random, wandering, shallow prayers, but intentional, serious prayers—like the ones you get out of the Bible itself.

Wanting God's best for our children and grandchildren has become a vital motivator in keeping us committed to praying together. We pray over our daughters, sons-in-law, and grandchildren. We intentionally and regularly call out the Word and will of God over their lives to provide protection for them, and we strongly encourage you to do the same for your family. We've seen the difference it can make and are confident it will make a difference in yours as well.

5. Growing in Understanding the Bible Together

> *All Scripture is God-breathed and is useful for teaching, rebuking, correcting and training in righteousness, so that the servant of God may be thoroughly equipped for every good work.*
>
> —2 TIMOTHY 3:16–17

This key verse indicates that all of Scripture is the result of the creative breath of God. Although penned by human writers, the Bible has a divine Author. That means the Bible instructs us in everything we need to know as children in His family in order to grow in spiritual and emotional maturity. There are a prodigious number of examples and exhortations in the New Testament regarding growth. For example:

❖ Hold on to our courage and the hope of which we boast (Hebrews 3:6).

❖ Stand firm (Philippians 1:27; 4:1).

❖ Continue in your faith, established and firm, not moved from the hope held out in the gospel (Colossians 1:23).

❖ Rooted and built up in Him, faith strengthened (Colossians 2:7).

✤ Boast about your perseverance and faith in all the persecutions and trials, which you are enduring (2 Thessalonians 1:4).

✤ Become mature, attaining to the whole measure of the fullness of Christ (Ephesians 4:13).

✤ No longer be infants, tossed back and forth by the waves, and blown here and there by every wind of teaching (Ephesians 4:14).

✤ Grow up into Him who is the head, that is Christ (Ephesians 4:15).

✤ Go on to maturity (Hebrews 6:1).

✤ But solid food is for the mature, who by constant use train themselves to distinguish good from evil (Hebrews 5:14).

✤ Do not merely listen to the word, and so deceive yourselves. Do what it says (James 1:22).

✤ May that great Shepherd of the sheep equip you with every good thing for doing His will, and may He work in us what is pleasing to him through Jesus Christ, to him be glory forever and ever! Amen (Hebrews 13:20–21).

As you and your spouse pray slowly through books of Bible you will grow spiritually—together! As you search for prayer content, God will unfold key words, phrases, concepts, and truths to nurture your souls. Praying the Bible will become an adhesive in your marriage.

While there certainly is great benefit and growth as you encounter the Word of God at church, in a Sunday School class, or in a small group study, the most intimate gathering of two or three who come together in Jesus' name is in your marriage.

"Do your best to present yourself to God as one approved, a worker who does not need to be ashamed and who correctly handles the word of truth" (2 Timothy 2:15). Praying the Word as co-workers with God will grow you in handling His truth.

6. Prayers "In the Name of Jesus"

Most of us are accustomed to closing our prayers with the phrase *"in Jesus' name."* But why? Is it some magic formula we include to get God's attention or coerce positive answer to our prayers? Are we mindlessly tacking on these routine words? No, and hopefully, no.

Praying in Jesus' name is powerful because it says several things to God:

(a) "Father, we affirm our sole approach to You is through Jesus our Savior."

We have no other valid access to the Father other than through Jesus who is the "way and the truth and the life" (John 14:6). Can you imagine coming before God in your own name? No way! We approach the Father in the name of the One and Only Son of God, because there is "one mediator between God and mankind, the man Christ Jesus, who gave himself as a ransom for all people" (1 Timothy 2:5-6). Without Jesus as our advocate and forerunner, we have no right to come to God.

(b) "Father, we do not presume with our own wants or perspective."

On our own, our prayers arise from a terribly limited perspective, and our hearts are often confused with selfishness. In line with Jesus' prayer of submission in the garden of Gethsemane, though, we aspire to have His attitude that "not my will, but Thy will be done" (Matthew 26:39, authors' paraphrase). To pray in Jesus' name affirms our humility and submission to God, and it affirms that He is God and we are certainly not! As we lift up our desires in Jesus' name, we position our hearts to acknowledge that God knows what is best.

(c) "Father, we submit this prayer, as if Jesus were praying it Himself."

We bring our prayers before the Father in such as way that Jesus would voice this very prayer Himself. As Scripture says, "We have a great high priest who has ascended into heaven, Jesus the Son of God, let us hold firmly to the faith we profess" (Hebrews 4:14).

By praying with the Bible as our guide, we are guaranteed to be praying "in Jesus' name." Our prayers and praises are in harmony with the will of our Advocate, Jesus Christ. We sense that our prayers are more "on target" because the more we pray in the path of God's Word and will, the more we are in harmony with Jesus' name.

7. Spirit of Anticipation

As of the writing of this book, we are praying through the Gospel of Mark and have actually been doing this for several months. It's taking us a while, but this is not a race, and we have no deadline. In the process, we notice that something fascinating has developed. We have begun to look forward to each prayertime, wondering, "What is the Lord going to show us to pray about today?"

When husbands and wives pray with no other agenda than what the Bible provides, prayer points emerge that become the content and focus of our prayertime. And that's pretty exciting! God always has more interesting ideas for prayer than we do.

Two examples jump to the forefront of how God has met each of us in very specific ways. One morning as we were about to read and pray in Mark, Sam said to Vicki, "I have a prayer request for you. Will you pray for my faith to be strengthened? I am sensing pressure concerning several issues that are producing some doubt in my heart and mind." We talked a bit more about some related details, then turned to where we were praying through the Gospel of Mark. It happened to be Mark 6:1–6, the story of Jesus returning to His hometown. After teaching there, people barraged Him with skeptical questioning, and the passage says the people took offense at Him! The final verse in the story says, "He was amazed at their lack of faith."

After reading that Scripture, we sat quiet for a moment. Then Vicki, with a wry smile on her face, asked Sam, "So, what do you see in this passage?"

Sam answered, "Well, I guess Jesus is amazed at my lack of faith." And we both burst into laughter!

It was the perfect story, at the perfect time, to confirm the issue at hand: faith! That morning, we prayed over the issue of faith for ourselves, our family, and our ministry with e3 Partners in Colombia.

Another time we were praying through the Book of Hebrews (which also took us several months, by the way). We came to Hebrews 13:7, which says, "Remember your leaders, who spoke the word of God to you. Consider the outcome of their way of life and imitate their faith." (Notice that in praying through Scripture, you are not trying to cover many verses. Often we read only a few verses at time, and in this case, just this one verse made a big difference in our prayer.)

Sam said, "Let's stop right here and do exactly that. Let's remember the leaders who spoke the Word of God into our lives."

This would be different from having heard a great sermon on the radio or having read an influential book. We thought back to the beginning of our Christian lives 40 years ago and took out a piece of paper. In short order, we jotted down the names of more than 40 people. The exercise was deeply meaningful to both of us, but it especially touched Vicki's heart when we prayed for these people.

Taking this trip down our spiritual memory lane reminded Vicki of how wonderfully God orchestrated His input into our lives. We listed the people who led us to the Lord, pastors and their wives, professors and teachers, close friends, mentors, even people from Romania and Colombia we served with on missions trips.

This was not an ordinary list of people. These were people God sent to run alongside of us in our race. They were cheerleaders and coaches, alike, people who not only loved us, but who loved our daughters as well. They each supported our ministry in some way, and as the passage says, "they spoke the word of God to us." The Word of God was the common denominator for them all. They not only taught us formally with the written Word, but they lived the Word with us and before us, and before our daughters.

It was a powerful and tearful time of prayer. We praised God for the outcome of their way of life and asked God to help us to imitate their faith. We prayed, "Dear Lord, we are asking You to use us in people's lives as You used this great company of your servants to fingerprint our lives." Even now, just recalling this exercise in prayer, it is deeply meaningful to remember what God has done for us.

We think you will be blessed if you try the same exercise. Read Hebrews 13:7, get out a piece of paper, and enjoy the journey back over your spiritual pilgrimage. Then praise God for the witnesses He set around your life, and ask Him for whom can you do the same.

A SUMMARY OF WHY TO PRAY THE BIBLE

Our prayers can be more dynamic and effective than aimlessly asking the Lord to "bless this and bless that." Our prayers will be energized by the Holy Spirit's guidance as we use the Bible as a prayer guide. We can follow the very things that concern the heart of God, for He wrote them down for us in His holy Word.

Because the Bible is the living and active Word of God and because the Holy Spirit is in each of us as believers in Jesus Christ, He is present to illuminate His Word to us. Although it does not happen every time, there are times as we are praying through books of the Bible that it becomes clear exactly what God wants us to pray about. Sam is not the leader of our prayertime, and neither is Vicki. We often look at each other, joyfully realizing that God truly is leading our prayertime!

Jesus said to the Jews who had believed in Him, "If you abide in My word, you are My disciples indeed" (John 8:31 NKJV). The word *abide* includes the ideas of "remaining, being at home; resting in." As we pray the Word, it takes a deeper place at home, in our lives, in our marriage, and in our family. And it becomes evident that we are truly Jesus' disciples.

PRAY TOGETHER

For the word of God is alive and active. Sharper than any double-edged sword, it penetrates even to dividing soul and spirit, joints and marrow; it judges the thoughts and attitudes of the heart. Nothing in all creation is hidden from God's sight. Everything is uncovered and laid bare before the eyes of him to whom we must give account.

—HEBREWS 4:12–13

Lord, Your Word is not a regular book but is a living and active Word, sharper than any double-edged sword. It has the power to penetrate into our souls and spirits and the ability to look deep inside and judge the thoughts and attitudes of our hearts. We confess that nothing is hidden from Your sight, God. Everything is open and revealed before Your eyes. Help us remember that we must give account for our lives. Praying through Your Word together, we are confident You will accomplish a deep work in our marriage and family according to Your will. Amen.

CHAPTER 10

BIBLICAL CORNERSTONES

I look forward to praying Scripture with my wife—we have decided to begin this practice together in large part because of your book. I ask for your prayers as we begin this journey of praying and reading the Word. We've been married for 11 years, and I dearly love my wife. I do my best to lead, but it can be a struggle from time to time. Shannon and I spend time praying together, but our times can be inconsistent and need to be more intentional. I am grateful to God for this book. It came at the perfect time for us in our marriage. Praise God for His goodness and thank you for writing this resource. Blessings.

—LARRY

What a great tool God has given to you! It pierced my heart and now is the motive of my main messages. I have been telling my friends about it. I hope to have more time now to put it in practice in my church. I am personally committed to it and the process, and I will teach some in Cuba this week. Thanks again!

—OMAR

During an intriguing radio interview, a divorce attorney shared his observation about which month of the year is most popular for filing divorce proceedings. He claimed there was a predictable annual pattern. As the end of the year approaches, it seems that a married couple may struggle with their commitment to stay together. With the holidays at hand, they determine it is better for the family to just get through the season without disruption. Once the calendar turns to January, though, they finalize the decision to split up. Then, during February, basic plans are formulated concerning what the new future will look like after the husband and wife go their separate ways. Which brings us to March—the month the lawyer said is when the most divorce proceedings are actually filed with the courts.

A HOUSE *UNDIVIDED*

Jesus said, "Every kingdom divided against itself will be ruined, and every city or household divided against itself will not stand" (Matthew 12:25). He made the pronouncement to the religious leaders of the Jews after they had accused Jesus of casting out demons by the power of Satan. They had said, "It is only by Beelzebul, the prince of demons, that this fellow drives out demons" (v. 24). In response, Jesus points out the senselessness of the accusation. His logic is clear. No kingdom, city, or household will survive—let alone flourish and grow—if it destroys itself. Self-destruction is the worst kind of demise.

Jesus referenced households in His rebuttal to the Jewish leaders, and while He did not specifically mention marriage, clearly the union of husband and wife is the engine of the household. If the engine is not functioning any longer, the marriage and the household will cease to move forward, and once the energy of a marriage is focused on dividing itself, it cannot stand.

One of the main goals of this book is to help Christian marriages stand firm even when opposition is fierce. In Chapter 9, we reviewed seven benefits of praying the Word of God in our marriages. Now we will look at seven biblical foundations that encourage praying the Word of God and solidify unity in the face of factors that otherwise might divide us. Although there are no specific verses in the Bible that command husbands and wives to pray together using the Word, we are convinced this path is a reasonable conclusion as evidenced by a host of Scriptures about the power of God's Word and the importance of the institution of marriage.

The seven benefits in Chapter 9 and the seven biblical foundations that follow are intended to convince and motivate you toward more intentional and more regular spiritual union in your marriage. May you resolve by God's grace that your marriage will not only stand, but it will grow in increasing health and maturity. A healthy, mature marriage strengthens its household, the city, and, ultimately, God's kingdom. Each foundation contributes to the vital model of praying through books of the Bible as a guide to our prayers in marriage. Before discussing each in detail, here is the topline summary:

1. MARITAL INTIMACY
   Genesis 2:24–25—Naked and Not Ashamed

2. GOD'S PRESENCE
   Matthew 18:20—There Am I with Them

3. CONFIDENT APPROACH
   Hebrews 4:14-16—The Throne of Grace

4. UNHINDERED PRAYERS
   1 Peter 3:7—So That Nothing Will Hinder Your Prayers

5. Useful Scripture

2 Timothy 3:16–17—All Scripture Is God-Breathed and Useful

6. Cleansing through the Word

Ephesians 5:25–28—Washing with the Word

7. Love and Respect

Ephesians 5:32–33—Love His Wife, Respect Her Husband

1. MARITAL INTIMACY

*For this reason a man shall leave his father and his mother,
and be joined to his wife; and they shall become one flesh.
And the man and his wife were both naked and were not
ashamed.*

—GENESIS 2:24–25 NASB

Shame

"You should be ashamed of yourself!"

Have you ever experienced these embarrassing words cast your way? Not so motivating, are they? In fact, they probably leave you feeling exposed, condemned, and perhaps even humiliated. Shame is a powerful force. When we come to grips with justifiable guilt, the feeling of shame can motivate us to make some needed changes in attitudes, perspectives, and behaviors. On the other hand, the feeling of shame can pronounce negative results without mercy. Shame not only points out something we did or said, but it nails us personally. Shame says you failed at something, and it goes on to say you are a failure as a person. Shamed people are deficient; they don't measure up; they are defective. The jury of whomever has returned to the courtroom to confirm our guilt—and to remind us that we are bad people! Shame arises from being exposed in the presence of another. Since we have been "found out," the tendency is to hide. It was the same with Adam and Eve.

Hiding in the Garden

God designed husband and wife to be "one flesh" in marriage. This oneness promotes a holistic intimacy that God identifies as nakedness. The nakedness consists of a natural transparency and vulnerability that leaves no space for shame. If only we could find our way back to the Garden of Eden!

You remember the story. Adam and Eve are living in complete harmony, innocence, and peacefulness in the presence of God. But when sin arrived, everything beautiful broke. They were no longer comfortable with their nakedness, so Adam and Eve gathered leaves and wove them into clothes to cover their physical nakedness. Then God arrived for their regular walk with Him, but shame beat Him there and drove the man and his wife to the bushes for cover.

Naked Prayer

When a husband and wife intentionally pray together, many great things can happen. The unique oneness of their marriage is affirmed and enhanced, and as we come before the Lord together, an atmosphere of humility arises. Prayertime fosters vulnerability and transparency before our holy God and before one another. Our hearts are increasingly "naked" and open to God and spouse. Self-focused personal agendas, and perceived rights take a backseat to serving the needs and desires of our spouse first. And most importantly, the dark side of shame is cast out. The need to hide is exchanged for honesty. Compassion and sensitivity increase.

Such benefits become evident in our marriage because:

> *Two are better than one, because they have a good return for their labor: If either of them falls down, one can help the other up. But pity anyone who falls and has no one to help them up. Also, if two lie down together, they will keep warm. But how can one keep warm alone? Though one may be overpowered, two can defend themselves. A cord of three strands is not quickly broken.*
>
> —ECCLESIASTES 4:9–12

This two-are-better-than-one principle is why the Bible calls us to pray with other Christians.

The disciples once asked Jesus for an important bit of instruction: "teach us to pray" (Luke 11:1). Over the centuries, His response has become known as the Lord's Prayer. And notice that each petition in the prayer is given in the plural: *our* Father, give *us*, lead *us*, deliver *us* (Matthew 6:9–13). Without question, there is the need for each believer to engage in personal and private prayer, yet there is enormous power in prayer with other believers—especially partners in life!

2. GOD'S PRESENCE

> *For where two or three gather in my name, there am I with them.*
>
> —MATTHEW 18:20

The presence of God is an important theme throughout the Bible. In the earliest chapters of Genesis, God walks in the cool of the garden with Adam and Eve, and at the other end—in Revelation 21—a new heaven and new earth is created and the holy city, the new Jerusalem comes down out of heaven after which a loud voice from the throne says, "Behold, the tabernacle of God *is* with men, and He will dwell with them, and they shall be His people. God Himself will be with them *and be* their God" (v. 3 NKJV). From one end of the Bible to the other, God intends to dwell with His people!

The phrase "I am with you" appears 21 times in the Bible. God affirms His presence with Jacob, Joshua, to and through Jeremiah and Isaiah, and generally to His people throughout the Old Testament. God's presence provides strength, help, protection, comfort, and security. Through His presence, God can save, rescue, and deliver. Our nemesis of fear is confronted and cast out as we embrace the reality of God's presence. Over and over, God says to His people, "Do not be afraid for I am with you."

Jesus specifically promises His presence in the final words before His ascension. His parting command is often called the Great Commission, but there are two significant "bookends" around His command to make disciples:

> (1) The Authority of Christ—"All authority in heaven and on earth has been given to me" (Matthew 28:18).

> (2) The Presence of Christ—"And surely I am with you always, to the very end of the age" (Matthew 28:20).

Jesus affirms that His presence equips and sustains our lives for the obedient service of making disciples.

One of the amazing teachings of the New Testament is the presence of God in each individual believer. Christ lives *in* us. We are the temple of the Holy Spirit. Of course, this is both comforting and convicting. He knows everything going on outside and inside of us! Yet the presence of God is also manifest in a special way as multiple believers come together. Jesus says, "Where two or three gather in my name, there am I with them" (Matthew 18:20).

It seems reasonable that the most intimate gathering of two would certainly be marriage. When we come together in Jesus' name, as a believing husband and wife, Jesus promises that He is present with us. The three-way partnership of marriage—husband, wife, and God—becomes a living reality. Praying as husband and wife both acknowledges and invites Jesus' presence in marriage, home, and family. By uniting together for prayer in the oneness of marriage, we gather in Jesus' name, and He promises to be present.

As we pray the Word, the presence of Jesus Christ not only comes to us through the Holy Spirit but through Scripture itself. Through it, we access the blessings and promises associated with the presence of God!

The presence of God may be a truth we take for granted, but as we are intentional and regular in marital prayer, His presence will come more to the forefront, bringing its attendant blessings. "So do not fear, for I am with you; do not be dismayed, for I am your God. I will strengthen you and help you; I will uphold you with my righteous right hand" (Isaiah 41:10).

3. CONFIDENT APPROACH

Therefore, since we have a great high priest who has ascended into heaven, Jesus the Son of God, let us hold firmly to the faith we profess. For we do not have a high priest who is unable to empathize with our weaknesses, but we have one who has been tempted in every way, just as we are—yet he did not sin. Let us then approach God's throne of grace with confidence, so that we may receive mercy and find grace to help us in our time of need.

—HEBREWS 4:14–16

This passage follows the one in which the writer to the Hebrews declares that the Word of God is living, active, sharp, and penetrating. The sharpness of the God's Word probes the immaterial part of our being. It divides the soul and judges the thoughts and attitudes of our heart. He concludes, "Nothing in all creation is hidden from God's sight. Everything is uncovered and laid bare before the eyes of him to whom we must give account" (Hebrews 4:13). We are continually exposed before a God who knows all things—past, present, and future. This reality is convicting—maybe even be scary for some of us. Although hiding is hardly an option, our innate sense of shame compels us to shrink back from God. How can we pray when He knows how unworthy and unqualified we are in our struggles, failures, and sins? It is possible to be paralyzed by our fears and failures.

Yet the writer of Hebrews has a "therefore" to share. There is more to the story. It's true: we cannot approach God on the merits of our worthiness. The beauty of the gospel is that God makes a way on our behalf based solely on the worthiness of His Son Jesus. We are reminded of several foundations undergirding our faith profession in Jesus Christ.

First, Jesus is our great high priest who has gone before us into the heavens. The essence of the high priest's role is to appear on behalf of those he represents. He is able to open the way that is otherwise shut off.

Secondly, Jesus is an understanding high priest. He sympathizes with our weaknesses. The Hebrews writer invites us to consider that Jesus was tempted in every way we are. But how can the holy Son of God be tempted? Theologians debate such matters in an attempt to "get around" teachings that are difficult to interpret, but we need not try to explain why the Bible does not mean what it clearly says. Jesus walked in this fallen world of sin. He was not only 100 percent God, but He was 100 percent man. He felt the pressure of evil. In fact, because of who He is, He may have felt it more readily than any other person.

A third anchor for our faith is something that was entirely different about Jesus in comparison with us. Sideswiped and shoved around by temptations as we are, at times, we inevitably fail—sometimes more than we care to think about. However, Jesus was entirely unique in that He was *without sin*. Jesus Christ is qualified not only by His role as our high priest, but more importantly by the perfect integrity of His character and being—He was and is entirely perfect!

The New Testament revelation in Jesus Christ and His gospel announces that God is *for us*! On our own, we fall short every time. But if we look at our sympathetic and sinless Savior, we can RSVP to God's invitation to "approach God's throne of grace with confidence."

Frequently, when people talk about confidence, it is positioned as being anchored in *self*. We are exhorted to exude *self*-confidence, *self*-reliance, and *self*-assurance. But the writer of Hebrews says that everything about *self* is exposed before God—and it's not a good source for confidence. Rather, our confidence is not in ourselves, but in our high priest Jesus Christ. We can confidently approach the throne of grace because Jesus has gone before us and invites us to follow. We are also reassured that Jesus serves as high priest, not only in providing access but also in personal intercession: "Therefore he is able to save completely those who come to God through him, because he always lives to intercede for them" (Hebrews 7:25).

The marvelous truth of the great throne of Christ is that there we may receive mercy and grace in time of need. And when is our time of need? *All the time*. Whether in marriage, family (both immediate and extended), place of work, decisions, pressures, losses, issues, or concerns and worries of life, we are continually in times of need.

God's throne of grace is the central place to which God calls us as individual Christians and in our marriages. There are many special places we may go together as husband and wife. It may be as simple as a date to your favorite restaurant or as exotic as an overseas vacation. But there is another place we should frequent as married couples, and it is more refreshing, peaceful, and satisfying than a mountain chalet or a beach-side condo, and the visit costs us nothing. We can be there in an instant, at any time of day or night. It is a place of union and communion with God, a place we can approach with confidence, thanks to Jesus: the throne of grace!

4. UNHINDERED PRAYERS

You husbands in the same way, live with your wives in an understanding way, as with someone weaker, since she is a woman; and show her honor as a fellow heir of the grace of life, so that your prayers will not be hindered.

—1 PETER 3:7 NASB

These words were revolutionary in the first-century Greco-Roman context. Normally, "standard marriage procedure" was to focus on the wife's responsibilities to her husband. Women generally were disrespected, and wives in particular were frequently treated as mere possessions. Peter pens God's inspired words, though, calling husbands to regard their wives with understanding, sensitivity, and honor. This was unheard of!

Throughout history, and even in some places today, many cultures and religions degrade women and regard them as inferior to men. They are treated like servants and as instruments to gratify a man's passions. For many years, even in many Western democracies, women were not given the right to vote. Christianity, though, confronts the injustice in such treatment and elevates women as coheirs of the grace, hope, and promises of Jesus Christ.

Wives are to be treated with respect, kindness, esteem, love, and honor. While Peter refers to the wife as a "someone who is weaker," the wife is not intellectually, emotionally, morally, or spiritually weaker. Peter contrasts her to the physical strength and power of a man's frame because, generally speaking, wives are more tender, delicate, fragile of structure, and subject to the fatigue and toils of life. On the other hand, can you imagine a man giving birth? No man who has witnessed a child being born would in his right mind claim, "I think I could handle that!"

Our marriages and homes are unique settings where esteem for womanhood can be on display. God clearly calls husbands to live with their wives in an understanding way. As Peter says, "Grant her honor." Why? Because she is a fellow heir of the grace of life.

Given that the goal of this book is to encourage marital prayer, there is an interesting and important connection to this granting of honor to a wife. Peter connects the husband's attitude and treatment of his wife to the *success of his prayers*. Peter warns that prayers may be hindered if the husband's attitude and treatment of his wife is not aligned with God's view. A man's perspective and treatment of his wife has serious spiritual implications.

The Lord calls a believing husband to grant honor to his wife as a fellow heir of the "grace of life." This giving of honor includes the emotional, spiritual, and even physical aspects of living. Intentional and regular prayers as husband and wife provide a dynamic setting for both understanding and honor to flow in a marriage. Guided by the Word of God, our prayers together:

* engage the spiritual attention and mutual respect required for successful marriage;

* bring relational contentment, peace, and love—which an abundance of money and possessions could never provide;

* cover our families and children with the Word and will of God; and

* strengthen the marriage to face the realities of life's trials, tests, losses, illnesses, and disappointments.

5. USEFUL SCRIPTURE

All Scripture is God-breathed and is useful for teaching, rebuking, correcting and training in righteousness, so that the servant of God may be thoroughly equipped for every good work.

—2 TIMOTHY 3:16–17

Near the early days of their second missionary journey, the Apostles Paul and Silas entered a city named Lystra. There, God provided a fellow traveler for their journey, a young man named Timothy, who was spoken well of by the brothers of the church. Timothy became a close companion and disciple of Paul's. The relationship was like a son serving with his father. It was so close, in fact, that to the Philippians, Paul said of Timothy, "I have no one else like him" (Philippians 2:20). The journey of their lives and service in planting and establishing churches wove their lives together with purpose and meaning. In fact, Paul's final epistles bear the name of Timothy.

The letter is rich concerning the reality of hard-hitting discipleship. Paul does not pull any punches as he rehearses for Timothy the extensive difficulties and darkness he was facing—not only in the path of ministry but personally as well. Paul was writing while literally held fast in Roman chains, yet the epistle shines bright with hope and expectation. The brief chapters are replete with truths and challenges that lift the reader's spirit to strength and endurance for kingdom business. The principle resource Paul brings before Timothy is the Holy Scriptures. Paul knew that from his infancy, Timothy had been raised under the influence of the Scriptures, apparently by his grandmother Lois and his mother Eunice.

"All Scripture is God-breathed," says Paul. The Bible in its entirety is the inspired Word of God. It is not an ordinary book written by men, but one given by the very breath of God through men He appointed to write. In its narrative stories, prophecies, doctrines, promises, psalms, and principles—in every phrase and every word, the Bible is the Word of God, and as such, it is "useful." Paul notes four areas in which the Word can be used for great benefit. *Teaching* is instruction with God's truths; *rebuking* and *correcting* identifies error and sinfulness, and points in the best direction; and *training* literally means child training. These vital functions of the Word compel us along the path of righteousness. The overall purpose is to thoroughly equip us for every good work.

Let the Bible to show you what to pray, instead of making up your prayers, on the spot, off the top of your head. Given what Paul says about the nature and usefulness of the Holy Scriptures, when we pray the Word of God out loud it will awaken in our hearts and minds. Our prayers awaken teaching, rebuking, correcting, and training in righteousness. Through our voicing the Word of God in prayer, God accomplishes a more thorough preparation for every good work He has planned for us.

Think of the possibilities and power of praying the Word out loud over the lives of our children and grandchildren! It can and will make a difference. As a married couple, you can pray the teaching, rebuking, correcting, training, and equipping ministries of the Holy Scriptures over the legacy of your family. The Scriptures impacted Timothy from his infancy, and the same dynamic can be birthed in the lives of our children and grandchildren.

6. CLEANSING THROUGH THE WORD

Husbands, love your wives, just as Christ loved the church and gave himself up for her to make her holy, cleansing her by the washing with water through the word, and to present her to himself as a radiant church, without stain or wrinkle or any other blemish, but holy and blameless. In this same way, husbands ought to love their wives as their own bodies. He who loves his wife loves himself.

—EPHESIANS 5:25–28

The five biblical foundations that we have addressed so far have broad application to the ministry of prayer for any believer. But these last two cornerstones relate specifically to the spiritual and emotional health of a Christian marriage. In the second half of Ephesians, there are multiple exhortations concerning Christian living:

❖ "live a life worthy of the calling you have received" (4:1);

❖ "become mature, attaining to the whole measure of the fullness of Christ" (4:13);

❖ "follow God's example, therefore, as dearly loved children and walk in the way of love" (5:1-2);

❖ "live as children of light" (5:8); and

❖ "be filled with the Spirit" (5:18).

Paul also presents the exhortation for husbands "love your wives" as evidence of what the Spirit-filled husband will look like.

On the day of the wedding ceremony, a husband is captured by a deep love for his beautiful bride. Jesus Christ also loves His bride, the Church. These familiar verses reveal amazing things regarding the scope of Jesus' great love for His bride.

❖ His intention—Jesus loved the Church

❖ His sacrifice—Jesus gave Himself up for her

❖ His purpose—To sanctify and cleanse her

❖ His method—By the washing of water with the Word

❖ His goal—That He might present her to Himself in all her glory, having no spot or wrinkle or any such thing, that she should be holy and blameless.

Paul points to Jesus' great love and sacrifice for His bride to illustrate the standard of how husbands are to love their wives. A husband may legitimately wonder, "How can I love my wife like that?"

The husband's resolve to come near his wife in spiritual intimacy becomes a perfect expression of such love. A wife feels loved and valued through the attention given by her husband to help her be spiritually nourished. The discouraging reality for many husbands is that they are fumbling the ball of spiritual intimacy. He may feel pressured by thinking he needs to bring new and unique spiritual insights and ideas to his wife, but as we've pointed out, such thinking is a mistake. Praying the Word together becomes a dynamic tool to enhance spiritual and emotional connection because it is not about what we as husbands bring to the table. It is about what God brings to us in the course of praying His Word.

Notice, too, that the Bible says Jesus cleanses His bride by the "washing with water through the word." That is exactly *how* a husband can love his wife. By praying through the Word of God, a man will be "washing her with the water of the Word." The Greek word used here for word is *rhema*, which means something that is uttered or spoken. While there are a variety of views as to what this utterance refers to, we suggest that praying through the Bible is a practical way to give voice, or utterance, to God's truths. By praying out loud together you utter the truths of God. The Word births hope as we pray. It is the Holy Spirit's instrument to effect blessing—and even radical change— to bring His guidance, restoration, and perspective that can infuse new life into our marriages, children, extended family, ministries, and careers. Praying the Word as a married couple invites a sanctifying, cleansing effect. Paul speaks directly concerning the impact on the wife's life, but the same effect influences the husband as well.

In our experience, praying the Word weaves the Word more intimately into our souls. It becomes more memorable, especially when the providential timing of God unites a current life issue with the content of the verses we are praying. "Cleansing her by the washing with the water through the word" invokes the symbol of being cleansed as we are baptized with the spoken Word. As we speak our way through the Word with prayers, Scripture washes us. This is not to say we are using God's Word for our own self-serving purposes. Rather, we allow God's Word to inform our prayers so as to invite God's purposes into our lives. The goal is not "my kingdom come" but "Thy kingdom come."

Paul calls husbands to the model of love that Jesus demonstrates by saying, "husbands ought to love their wives." He goes on to say, "In this same way, husbands ought to love their wives as their own bodies. He who loves his wife loves himself." "In this same way," means that Jesus' love for His bride is not only an example of love to behold, but also a model to follow. By the grace of God, a husband can embrace the challenge and opportunity to step toward improved spiritual leadership in his marriage. We pray this encourages you to pursue this very path!

Jesus' gospel creates the foundation, and His ongoing work in our lives focuses on increasing our godliness. He desires to build for Himself, a church who is radiant, without stain, wrinkle, or blemish, holy and blameless. Praying the Word as husband and wife is a practical way to move each of us forward in this work of sanctification.

7. LOVE AND RESPECT

This is a profound mystery—but I am talking about Christ and the church. However, each one of you also must love his wife as he loves himself, and the wife must respect her husband.

—EPHESIANS 5:32–33

Paul concludes Ephesians 5 concerning Spirit-filled marriage with clear and practical commands. Husbands are commanded to love their wives. Wives are commanded to respect their husbands.

Paul reaches back to Genesis 2:24-25 to remind his readers that the husband and wife are "one flesh" (Ephesians 5:31). This represents a mystery, which is rich with far-reaching implications and importance. There is a powerful parallel between the oneness and intimacy of Christ with His Church and the believing husband with his wife. Certainly, husband and wife retain their individual identities, roles, and accountability, yet simultaneously they are woven as one. The result is not uniformity and sameness but, rather, unity and togetherness.

Marriage is God's provision for man and woman to experience the beauty and resources of the most intimate relationship among human beings. God did not create a parent and child in the garden; He created a husband and a wife. The marriage union is the engine of a strong family and the core of healthy society. We should not be shocked at the intense and directed pressure on the institution of marriage. As marriage is demeaned, redefined, and minimized in importance, the family—and in turn, society—is severely damaged. The enemy of our souls is delighted to see his agenda to steal, kill, and destroy being advanced.

In stark contrast, Jesus Christ loves and cares for the Church because it is the body of Christ. She does not only *represent* Jesus in the community; she *is* Jesus' presence in the community. This parallel demonstrates the extent to which each husband is to love his wife: he must love his wife as he loves himself! Previously in this chapter Paul writes, "Husbands ought to love their wives as their own bodies. He who loves his wife loves himself. After all, no one ever hated their own body, but they feed and care for their body" (5:28–29). It is natural and healthy for a husband to attend to the needs of his body, and since the wife is one with her husband (and this is illustrated in the union of physical intimacy), it is most natural and healthy for the husband to care for his wife.

How is this important relationship best nurtured? Let's look at a tasty analogy.

People love a good cup of piping-hot coffee in the morning. For many, their preferred way to drink coffee is to have it flavored with just the right balance of two extra ingredients: cream and sugar. Likewise, it takes the balance of two key ingredients to flavor a healthy marriage: love and respect. As the husband loves his wife, she is inspired toward respecting him. As the wife respects her husband, the husband is motivated to love her. The flow of these mutual expressions has a reciprocal and increasing impact on the marriage. More love and more respect yields more respect and more love!

To test the accuracy of this, we have, from time to time, asked couples to complete a brief marriage quiz. You might want to try this on yourself or some of your friends. Ask a husband if he would rather have his wife tell him, "I love you" or "I am proud of you." Most will pick "I am proud of you!" But ask a wife if she would rather hear husband say, "Honey, I love you" or "Honey, I am proud of you," and many will say they prefer to hear "I love you."

Even so, Paul's exhortation is not exclusive. The reverse expression of these virtues applies in healthy marriages. Wives should love their husbands, and husbands should be proud of their wives. Yet Paul strikes the primary chord in the DNA of each gender to fuel Spirit-filled and growing intimacy in marriage.

The virtues of love and respect charge the atmosphere with positive energy and joy. When we are more intentional in praying together, love and respect are cultivated in our hearts toward one another. As a husband prays through the Word, his wife witnesses her husband's humility before the Lord, sensitivity to what they are facing in life, and his attention to her soul—and her respect for him escalates. As the wife prays the Word, the husband increasingly learns how God speaks to her heart and how she voices her praises and requests—and his love for her increases in tenderness and understanding. Spirit-filled love and respect build upon one another lifting up every other dimension of marriage and family.

PRAY TOGETHER

All Scripture is God-breathed and is useful for teaching, rebuking, correcting and training in righteousness, so that the servant of God may be thoroughly equipped for every good work.

—2 TIMOTHY 3:16–17

Our Father, we are reminded about the nature and character of Your holy Word—that all of Scripture is inspired by Your very breath! We believe the Bible is no ordinary book from ancient times, but it is Your fresh Word every day. As we are learning to pray with the Word of God as our guide, we acknowledge that it is useful for teaching, rebuking, correcting, and training in righteousness. We are Your servants, God, and we are grateful that Your will is to thoroughly equip us for every good work You have prepared for us to accomplish! Amen.

CASTING SEEDS OF HOPE

My wife and I started regular prayer together more than a year ago, and it is a life changer. It certainly helps take marriage to the next level. We have floundered a bit in finding something to center our time around, and your suggestion of praying the Bible seems spot on. . . . I intend to take this to the men of our church.

—TOM

Some of the most transformative ideas are the most obvious ones. I have served as a pastor and now as a missionary. As such, I pour much of my time and energy into others. I often fall into the trap of neglecting to pray for and read Scripture with my wife. I do this to my peril. This model of praying Scripture is a wonderfully simple reminder of the transformative power of prayer and Scripture in marriage and ministry.

—JEFF

One Saturday morning, we enjoyed the opportunity to speak on marital prayer to 70 couples during a marriage seminar at a church in our community. Over the years, the sponsoring church had been acknowledged as a flagship church in the city, so we were humbled at the opportunity, and a bit nervous. Yet we also sensed an increasing enthusiasm as the date approached. We were slowly praying through the Book of Colossians, and two days before the event, we providentially came to these verses:

> *Devote yourselves to prayer, being watchful and thankful. And pray for us, too, that God may open a door for our message, so that we may proclaim the mystery of Christ, for which I am in chains. Pray that I may proclaim it clearly, as I should. Be wise in the way you act toward outsiders; make the most of every opportunity. Let your conversation be always full of grace, seasoned with salt, so that you may know how to answer everyone.*
>
> —COLOSSIANS 4:2–6

As you can see, there were a number of words and phrases in this passage that had direct bearing upon how we were feeling and what we needed at this very time:

❖ Devotion to prayer
❖ An open door for our message
❖ Proclaiming the mystery of Christ
❖ Clarity of message
❖ Wisdom
❖ Making the most of the opportunity
❖ Gracious conversation
❖ Knowing how to answer everyone

These truths from the Bible were timely and a perfect guide for our prayers as we prepared for the seminar.

This was an especially exciting example of how God meets us in prayer. Certainly, it is not quite so clear-cut every time we pray together, but whether we know it or feel it, we are confident God is with us in a special way, using this spiritual discipline to draw us closer to Him and to one another.

SOWING IN HOPE OF A HARVEST

We arrived early for our presentation to set up and be available to meet and greet the couples as they arrived. The atmosphere was energetic—smiles all around, and the room was full.

The range of attendees was exciting, too. One couple were newlyweds of only seven months. An elderly couple had just celebrated their sixtieth wedding anniversary! And they were others everywhere in between. We opened our talk by asking, "Are there any marriage experts in the room?" As intended, the rhetorical question elicited a rousing round of laughter.

We imagined that many of these couples are happily married, raising their families, enjoying the blessings and provision of God and loving their church. However, another thought came to us as we prepared for the seminar. Lurking behind the closed doors of the 70 Christian homes represented by these marriages was likely every kind of problem, trouble, trial, sin, pressure, and stress that we could imagine. Life is real, and reality is difficult—yes, even for Christians, our families, and our marriages. Some were likely battling the stress of insufficient finances, pressures with small children, instability and uncertainty about what to do with their teenagers, persistent illnesses, difficulties with in-laws, sexual tensions and haunting emotional wounds, workaholism, alcoholism, unemployment, anger issues, and at the epicenter of all of the issues: the inability to communicate well. Does our speculation ring true? Yet these married couples in Christ were not attending as hypocrites but as hope-seekers!

What seed, we wondered, *could we sow to the varied soils of these marriages in order to influence them positively? What could we possibly give them in a few hours on Saturday morning that would inject their souls, not with weighty guilt but with anticipation and hope? Is there a simple, reasonable path that could apply to each and every marriage, regardless of the troubles they were juggling? Could they walk away holding hands and with a new brightness in their eyes?* We deeply hoped that whatever we shared would bear great fruit in the lives before us.

THE BEST OF SPIRITUAL INTENTIONS

There are many ways to foster the life and health of spiritual intimacy in our marriages. Marital prayer with the Bible as your guide may not be the only way, but we do know this path can be core to touching your marriage deeply. On that Saturday we knew we could not touch every issue that a collection of 70 marriages struggles with, but we knew of Someone who could touch each one of those issues personally, with the most perfect timing if we could just help the folks find the path to allowing that Someone to help.

As we shared earlier, Peter wrote, "Come near to God and he will come near to you" (James 4:8). The dynamic of the marital trinity comes to a fresh and energized life and vitality when we draw near to God together. The three-strand rope of marriage, prayer, and the Word of God creates strength.

As you consider launching into this adventure yourselves, look at the Appendix, "Praying through the Book of James." The model for how to pray through a book may well help you take the first step on a journey you'll rejoice in for the rest of your lives!

PRAY TOGETHER

Two are better than one, because they have a good return for their labor: If either of them falls down, one can help the other up. But pity anyone who falls and has no one to help them up. Also, if two lie down together, they will keep warm. But how can one keep warm alone? Though one may be overpowered, two can defend themselves. A cord of three strands is not quickly broken.

—ECCLESIASTES 4:9–12

Father, we thank You for our marriage! We honor the truth that You have ordained that we be together, for we know that two are, indeed, better than one. There is good return as we labor in life together; we can help one another in times of failure because, clearly, we all stumble at times. We praise You for the warmth of being together and for the strength we have together to defend our marriage and family against the assaults of this world. We acknowledge this great truth that "a cord of three strands is not quickly broken." You, God, are our Father, Savior, and Lord, and we are blessed that Your very life weaves our marriage together into an increasingly strong and durable cord. Amen.

PRAYING THROUGH
THE BOOK OF JAMES

We've prepared this prayer plan to help you read and pray through the New Testament Book of James. Our purpose is to present a model of prayer that enables husbands and wives to pray together more consistently and effectively. The Bible is the living and active Word of God; therefore, praying through Scripture becomes a practical way to draw God's Word into your life, marriage, and family. This guide provides a selection of verses for each prayertime that will take you through the entire Book of James. It also offers a suggested prayer that expresses several main ideas from the verses. We are merely seeking to provide a sample prayer for each section but suggest you pray whatever the Lord shows you as husband and wife from each section of verses.

PRACTICAL REMINDERS

Once you pray through the Book of James, we are confident you will be equipped to move on and pray through other books of the Bible together. As you do, you might benefit from a few practical suggestions that we have discovered in the years since we first started praying Scripture together.

1. Read the selection of verses you desire to pray through.
Don't cover too many verses at a time. Modern Bible versions often divide the text into sections with headings. This may prove helpful as you determine how many verses to read and pray over. Do one section at a time, and take turns reading the Bible, or approach it in whatever way is most workable for your marriage. We recommend that husband and wife each have a copy of the Bible, and use the same version of Scripture.

2. After reading, quietly think about the verses.
What jumps out at you? The Holy Spirit will show you the main ideas, words, topics, and concepts in the passage. You might mark them in your Bibles or jot them down on a piece of paper. Remember, the focus is seeking content for your prayers. What are you prompted to pray, considering what you see in these Scriptures?

3. **Briefly share with one another what you observe and what you sense you are hearing from the Holy Spirit.**
Remember, this is not a Bible study and teaching time. It is a *prayertime*. Allow the Bible to show you what to pray over your individual lives, marriage, children, church, ministry, and career. Also pray for other people as God leads you, weaving in the prayer ideas from the verses that may apply.

Bear in mind that, from time to time, you will come to a passage that is difficult to understand. At such times, simply see what key words or ideas may prompt a direction for your prayers.

4. **Take turns praying.**
Both husband and wife can voice a prayer to the Lord. Follow the flow of the verses in your prayers. Lift your heart to the Lord following the key words, ideas, phrases, topics, and content you see. Another way to approach praying through Scripture is to turn the verses into prayers. You may literally read the verses word for word in a prayerful spirit—in essence praying the very Words of God back to the Lord. Another approach we have found helpful is to alternate praying through the selection of verses. The husband prays through the first verse, the wife prays through the second verse, the husband prays through the third, the wife prays the fourth verse. Continue alternating praying through as many verses as you have selected. With every approach, do what is comfortable, most natural, and workable for the two of you.

As you continue praying together, you will both find increasing comfort and confidence in your communication with one another and with the Lord. May God bless your new journey of spiritual intimacy in your marriage!

USING JAMES AS YOUR PRAYER BOOK

Read James 1:1–8, then pray together.
Lord, these verses are easy to read but are difficult to live. We ask You to lift our perspective so we may consider it pure joy when we face trials of many kinds. Because we know that You desire to produce perseverance through the testing of our faith, let perseverance finish its work, so we may be mature and complete, not lacking anything! And during times of testing, we ask You to give us generously the wisdom we need so we do not experience the instability of being blown and tossed by seas and winds of doubt. Amen.

Read James 1:9–12, then pray together.
Father, we confess that You are our heavenly provider, and all of our earthly possessions come from Your gracious hand. We thank You for the high

position we have as believers in Jesus Christ. Our value and worth has nothing to do with what we possess materially, but is based upon who we are in Jesus! Material wealth is relative, fading, and, ultimately, will be destroyed. Help us, Lord, to hold it loosely and not trust in riches for our security or personal value. Keep our eyes fixed on eternal rewards, like the crown of life, which You have promised to those who love You. Amen.

Read James 1:13–15, then pray together.
Lord, we sense the pressure of living in a sinful world. We can be confused about the source of our temptations, but, God, we know You are not the one who tempts us. We are tempted when we are dragged away and enticed by our own evil desires that live in us as sinners. Temptation can be like a fishing lure that looks attractive but always has a hook in it. We recognize that sinful desire is conceived gives birth to sin, and sin, when it is full-grown, gives birth to death. Lord God, we ask for Your protection over our marriage and family in this crucial spiritual battle. Amen.

Read James 1:16–18, then pray together.
Lord, we ask You to guard our hearts from deception. We also ask You to protect the hearts of our children from deception, whether they be young or older. We are blessed that You are a giving God. You are the one who gives us every good and perfect gift. We have received countless gifts from You, for which we are filled with thanksgiving! Lord, we are also blessed to know that You do not change like shifting shadows. We know you are the same every day. Thank you, also, for choosing to give spiritual birth through the Word of Your truth, so that we can bear fruit for Your glory! Amen.

Read James 1:19–21, then pray together.
Lord, we pray over our marriage and over our children that we will be quick to listen—quick to listen to You, quick to listen to one another, quick to listen to people in our sphere of influence. We also need to be slow to speak. When people talk to us, help us not to be thinking about what we want to say. We ask You to move in our hearts to check human anger, which is so quick to flare up at times. We confess with Your Word that human anger does not produce the righteousness You desire. Also, guard us from embracing moral filth and the evil that is so available in the world around us. Please cultivate fertile soil in our hearts that can humbly accept the Word that has been planted in us! Amen.

Read James 1:22–25, then pray together.
Lord, every day mirrors are very useful to us, and James reminds us that Your

Word is like a mirror. We need to not only listen to the Word but to do what it says. If we only hear the Word and do not obey the Word, it is like looking in a mirror and ignoring the things that are out of order. When we see the need for corrections and changes, give us the courage to intentionally address them. Your perfect law is not about legalism, but it is about freedom—freedom to obey You out of love. Because when we obey You out of love, we will be blessed in that beautiful path! Amen.

Read James 1:26–27, then pray together.

Father, equip us to experience increasing success at keeping a tight rein on our tongues. When our tongues get out of control, we not only can hurt others, but we ultimately harm ourselves through words that can cause self-deception. Pure and faultless religion is realized when we serve distressed people such as orphans and widows. Sharpen our awareness to observe and help such needy people you bring into our lives. We recognize that the world is polluted with sin, so protect our marriage and our children from the infection of sinful influences. Incline our hearts toward holy choices that are reflected in clear and regular obedience. Amen.

Read James 2:1–4, then pray together.

The phrase "brothers and sisters" tells us that we are siblings in a spiritual family because we are believers in the Lord Jesus Christ. Living in Your spiritual family has responsibility and accountability for how we regard and treat people. Prejudice is a relevant issue, because we are so easily disposed to making judgments based upon outward appearances and material things. Please guard our hearts and minds from judging with evil thoughts. We humbly confess to You, God, that we are easily given to judgments. May we not even see categories of "rich or poor." We ask you to "lift our eyes to see what you see" when we look at people. Amen.

Read James 2:5–7, then pray together.

Lord, guard our hearts and our judgments in all of our relationships: in the community, at church, at work, and especially in our family. People should not be judged by appearance and possessions but regarded as God regards them, based on personal character and relationship with God. Remind us that the poor in the eyes of the world are often rich in faith and are blessed to inherit the kingdom of God. Often, wealthy people can be wrapped in arrogance as they exploit others, drag them to court, and blaspheme the name of God. Regardless of material possessions, what matters is character and relationship with God! Amen.

Read James 2:8–13, then pray together.

Jesus, You said the greatest and first commandment is to love God with all of our heart, soul, mind, and strength. You also said, "You shall love your neighbor as yourself." You are our King, and we seek to live by Your royal law. Protect our hearts from favoritism and judgments. Help us treat others' concerns as if they are as important as our own. Guide us, Lord, to speak and act as people who will be judged by the law that gives freedom. We plead Your mercy over us so we can become channels of Your mercy toward other people. Free us from competition, measuring, and judging. Amen.

Read James 2:14–19, then pray together.

Father, the clearest evidence of genuine faith is to produce good deeds. We do not want our faith to be useless but useful. Please show us how to invest our time, talents, and treasure for Your kingdom. Open our eyes afresh, and open the doors for us to touch the lives of people. Claiming to have faith alone is not enough. We seek a faith expressed in deeds! The demons believe in You, God, but they certainly are not serving You. May our faith pass the test of authenticity by flowing forth into actions of mercy, love, and sacrifice. Amen!

Read James 2:20–26, then pray together.

Lord, among the key balances You desire for our spiritual lives is faith and deeds. Abraham and Rahab are great examples. They were very different people, but both demonstrated genuine, bold, and obedient faith. A man and a woman—the father of the Jews and a Gentile, a patriarch and a prostitute! Abraham's faith and actions worked in perfect balance when he offered his son Isaac in obedience to You. And such genuine faith was credited to him as righteousness. Thank You, Lord! Rahab was considered righteous as she received and hid the Jewish spies in Jericho. We are grateful for these amazing examples of faith and works operating in perfect balance. We pray You grant us such balance in our lives with You. Amen.

Read James 3:1–6, then pray together.

Today, Your Word is calling us to the daily need to watch over the words of our tongues. A small bit placed in the mouth can turn a strong horse, and a massive ship is driven by powerful winds across the seas but steered by a very small rudder. We see that, in the same way, our tongues are only small members of the body, but they can make great boasts. A small spark starts an entire forest fire. And our tongues can also be as a fire. This is a sober reminder of how many times we have seen great trouble and strife launched by only a few ill-advised words. We ask You, Holy Spirit, to guard the words of our mouths. Amen.

Read James 3:7–12, then pray together.
Lord, James says that it can be easier to tame an animal than to tame the tongue. From our mouths can potentially come praising as well as cursing. But that is not how we want to be. How can the same spring bring forth both fresh water and salt water? A fig tree cannot bear olives, and a grapevine cannot bear figs. Such results are a contradiction. Lord, we are guilty from time to time of letting our words get ahead of our heads and even our hearts. So today, we particularly ask You to help us be examples of using healthy words for our children. May our home be a place of verbal peace! And when the occasions for difficult conversations arise, give us self-control, grace, and patience. Amen.

Read James 3:13–18, then pray together.
Father, today we pray over two important virtues of spiritual relationship: wisdom and peace. A good life is shown by deeds done in humility, which come from wisdom. Please guard our hearts from harboring bitter envy and selfish ambition—such attitudes are earthly, unspiritual, and even demonic. Teach us the wisdom that comes from heaven, which is pure, peace-loving, considerate, submissive, full of mercy and good fruit, impartial, and sincere. When we sow in peace we will reap a harvest of righteousness, but if we sow in envy and selfishness, we will reap accordingly. Grant us, Lord, a righteous harvest. Amen.

Read James 4:1–3, then pray together.
Lord, we realize there are vulnerabilities in marriage. There can be seasons of tension, fighting, and quarreling. Yet Jesus said, "A house divided against itself cannot stand." In times of disagreement, we ask You to grant us self-control to look into our own hearts and motives. Remind us that sometimes we have not because we ask not, and when we make requests of You and one another, give us the right motives. We pray, God, that You posture our hearts to seek the Spirit of wisdom and peace in our marriage and home. Amen.

Read James 4:4–6, then pray together.
Friendship with the system of this world brings us into spiritual adultery and causes us to be Your enemy. So, please guide us to choose carefully the allegiances and alliances of our lives. Your Holy Spirit dwells in our lives because we are Your children. You are a jealous God, and You long for the fellowship of Your Spirit within our lives. We confess that we are in a struggle between the world and the Spirit, and that we need your grace. God, You are opposed to the proud, but You give Your favor to the humble. Therefore, we ask Your Holy Spirit to grace our life with humility so our friendship and fellowship will be with You as our Father. Amen.

Read James 4:7–10, then pray together.
Father, strengthen us to resist the devil, and we claim the promise that he will flee from us. We seek to come near to You and know You will respond by coming near to us. We "wash our hands" and ask You to purify our hearts because we struggle with being double-minded. Grant us repentance to confront our struggle with sin so that we will grieve, mourn, wail, change our laughter to mourning, and our joy to gloom. We humble ourselves before You as our holy Lord and God. We praise You, Lord, that in our submission and brokenness You find the humility You are seeking in our lives, and then You promise to lift us up. Amen.

Read James 4:11–12, then pray together.
We tend easily toward the sin of comparing and contrasting ourselves with other people. If we view them "higher," we can be filled with jealousy and self-pity. If we view them "lower" than ourselves, then we are tempted to be overcome with pride. Your command is for us to love our neighbors and not to slander them and not to judge them. Awaken us to realize that making comparisons and contrasts among our brothers and sisters is the same as making judgments. Our responsibility is to love people and not judge them. There is only one Lawgiver and only one Judge, and we are not He! Amen.

Read James 4:13–17, then pray together.
We declare that "if the Lord wills, we will live and do this or that." We believe it is proper to be wise managers of our lives. However, we confess that our plans are completely in Your hands and under Your will. Clearly, we do not know what will happen tomorrow. Often we have been surprised or even felt side-swiped by things that have occurred to us. Our lives are a mist, which appears for a little while, and then we vanish. So guard our hearts and minds from arrogant and selfish scheming. Protect us from boasting, which is evil. When we know to do good, strengthen us, Lord to make the right choices with a submissive and humble spirit. Amen.

Read James 5:1–6, then pray together.
Lord, it is easy to fall into this trap of pursuing wealth and putting our trust in riches. Help us to honestly discern our attitudes toward possessions and wealth. In their temporary nature, they can rot, corrode, and be eaten away. Wealth can tempt us to treat people unjustly, as in the case of failing to pay workers their just wages, and riches can lure us into the false ease of luxury and self-indulgence. We want to acknowledge that everything we have has come from Your gracious hand. You are the ultimate Giver and Owner of all things.

We ask You this day to protect our hearts from the deceitfulness of riches! Amen.

Read James 5:7–9, then pray together.
Our Father, we believe the Lord Jesus is coming a second time to this earth, as the great King of kings and Lord of lords—and as the Judge! Please give us the virtue of patience as we await Jesus' return—just as a farmer waits for the land to yield its valuable crop and also waits for the autumn and spring rains. Equip us to stand firm, because the Lord's coming is near. Guard our hearts from focusing on people in an unhealthy way that causes us to grumble because of our foolish and ill-informed judgments. Give us hearts filled with faith and confident expectation about the reality of the return of the Lord. And please make us both ready! Amen.

Read James 5:10–12, then pray together.
Oh, Lord, our culture seems to breed impatience. We want things immediately and don't want anything to hinder our goals and plans. We need patience in the normal path of life, but these verses also introduce the reality of suffering. Your prophets are great examples of patience and perseverance, even in the face of suffering. Job suffered great losses and struggled in confusion, yet You ultimately enlightened his perspective and restored him beyond his original blessings! In times of suffering, help us remember that You are full of compassion and mercy. Guard us from swearing oaths, when all we need to say is a simple "yes" or "no" to guard the integrity of our hearts. Amen.

Read James 5:13–16, then pray together.
Father, when we have ongoing troubles—whether defeats, weaknesses, or sicknesses—remind us to pray! In times of blessing, may we pray songs of praise to You. Give us opportunity to pray with our spiritual leaders for healing—whether the sickness is emotional, spiritual, or physical. Open our hearts to confessing our sins to one another, for we realize that sin loves darkness and wants to remain hidden. But when it is confessed and exposed to the light, it loses its power over us. We believe the prayers of a righteous person are powerful and effective because he or she walks close with You in discernment. Help us be righteous people in You! Amen.

Read James 5:17–20, then pray together.
We thank You for an example in Elijah who experienced powerful and confident answers to fervent prayers. He was a human being, even as we are, so we receive the promise that we, too, can pray earnestly for God to things that

are undeniably beyond our control. Lord, open our eyes and hearts to people around us who are struggling and who may even be trapped in sin. Fill us with love and compassion instead of judgment. Show us how to extend a hand of rescue to hurting people, to see death and loss stopped, and to witness a multitude of sins covered by Your grace!

Lord, we thank You for helping us to be more intentional and more regular than we have ever been in praying together in our marriage. This has been a rich blessing to each of us and at the same time has certainly continued to be a challenge. Even if we have done well in praying consistently so far, please help us to remain vigilant and to continue. In fact, we ask that You show us which Bible book we should pray through next. Amen!

OTHER RESOURCES TO HELP

FUEL YOUR PRAYER LIFE

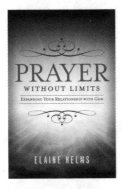

Prayer Without Limits
ELAINE HELMS
$14.99

978-1-59669-428-6

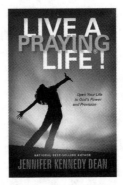

Live a Praying Life®
JENNIFER KENNEDY DEAN
$14.99

978-1-59669-436-1

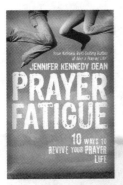

Prayer Fatigue

JENNIFER KENNEDY DEAN

978-1-59669-426-2

$15.99

To sample a free excerpt, learn more about these authors,
and for other prayer resources, visit
NewHopePublishers.com.